# LOVE
## UNLEASHED

# LOVE
# UNLEASHED

## Tales of Inspiration and the Life-Changing Power of Dogs

Rebecca Ascher-Walsh

NATIONAL GEOGRAPHIC

Washington, D.C.

DOUBLE TROUBLE: *Nora the English pointer was rescued from a puppy mill but never lost her sense of fun. She plays the loyal sidekick on adventures with her new human siblings.*

# CONTENTS

# INTRODUCTION

This is the third book I've written about extraordinary dogs for National Geographic, which means, as far as I'm concerned, that I have the best job in the world. Over the course of writing the other books—*Devoted* and *Loyal* before this—I have fallen in love time after time with the animals, and I made lasting friendships with many of the equally extraordinary humans with whom they are associated.

It has been a privilege from the first chapter of the first book to witness how these dogs are changing lives. And as someone who volunteers at my local shelter and heads a foundation that supports adoptions from shelters, I am always happy when the featured dogs happen to have been rescued. With *Love Unleashed*, I no longer relied on happenstance to find such dogs, but instead I sought them out. The narrative arc of a rescued dog who goes on to greatness—whether as a service dog or a steadfast companion—is inherently dramatic. But for me, these stories are also powerful—and poignant—illustrations of the themes that are most important to us as human beings: recognizing potential and keeping the faith.

Here, that looks like Brad Croft, the founder of Universal K9 and a trainer for dogs bred for law enforcement agencies. He recognized that too many dogs were dying in the Texas shelters near him. He also knew that in many cases, the high energy that didn't make them good pets was a hallmark of a glorious work ethic, and he could show them the way. He's now placing dogs like Libby the pit bull who works as a drug-sniffer for a Texas police department. Croft's charges are now performing as well as purchased pure breeds when it comes to narcotic and bomb detection.

It is also about people like Courtney Dasher, who adopted a funny-looking Chiweenie named Tuna who, due to a jaw abnormality, would likely have been overlooked in a shelter. Dasher began posting pictures of Tuna's special smile to Instagram, and the former under-dog is now a social media star with nearly two million fans. And there's Hattie Mae, a Labra-dor mix whose missing foot made her feel like a soul mate to a little girl who lost a leg at the age of nine. The best friends who met by chance have become sources of inspiration, not only to each other but to everyone around them.

Yes, *Love Unleashed* is about the dogs, but they wouldn't be here were it not for the humans on the other end of the leash—people who saw what the dogs could be. Here's to the magic of potential. Here's to keeping the faith. ◆

TRUE FRIENDS: *Author Rebecca Ascher-Walsh with her pit bull Buddy, one of two rescue dogs in her home who inspired her to found a nonprofit organization that aids pit bulls in need of adoption.*

PROUD PAPA: *When orphaned animals at the Cincinnati Zoo need a constant caretaker, Blakely steps in. Savanna the cheetah cub was the first charge he helped raise.*

# BLAKELY

## REDEFINING FAMILY

**Australian shepherd ⋅—⋅ Ohio**

**B**lakely is a four-legged lesson in compassion for those who are different. As a nursery companion dog raising orphaned infant animals into well-adjusted adults at the Cincinnati Zoo, he has cared for cheetahs, ocelots, a wallaby, a bat-eared fox, a serval, a takin, and even a warthog.

Blakely's babysitting services aren't just helpful to the zookeepers; they can be life-saving for orphaned animals who are unable to learn survival skills from their mothers. "If an animal is snarling at another who hasn't been taught to understand that it means back off, they can be killed," explains Dawn Strasser, the Cincinnati Zoo's head nursery keeper. Blakely teaches the nursery-bound babies the social skills that they need to thrive, and he comforts them while they sleep.

The beloved Blakely has been at the zoo since he himself was a pup. Strasser rescued him when he was six months old, and the cattle dog lived with a zoo volunteer until he proved that he had the docile temperament to be a caretaker. Since then, he's lived in the nursery helping Strasser and her colleague Michelle Kuchle, who both occasionally spend the night there. Otherwise, Blakely is in charge of the place, and even though he has a separate room to sleep in if he wants privacy, he usually pulls a dog bed in front of the babies' incubators or enclosures.

Blakely has cared for orphaned cheetah cubs who are part of the zoo's endangered species breeding and conservation program. In the beginning, Blakely would lie nervously in Strasser's lap while a cheetah cub crawled on him, but soon his paternal nature took over. The newborns mostly wanted to cuddle with Blakely, but as they grew, play became more important. Blakely taught them when to initiate play and when to end it. "If they got *too* rough, he corrected them," Strasser explains. Leading by example and interacting with the cheetahs as needed, Blakely taught them basic survival skills for six months until they were ready to live on their own.

## "HE KNEW EXACTLY WHAT TO DO, THANKS TO BLAKELY."

One of Blakely's greatest successes is an unlikely friend named Dale. The takin—a vulnerable species related to sheep—was placed in the nursery when he and his mother were not successfully bonding. "At birth, Dale was the size of Blakely," remembers the zoo's director Thane Maynard. "And pretty quickly he was four times as big." For four months, the duo continued to sleep, play, and even walk the zoo grounds together. When Dale eventually returned to his mother, Strasser remembers, he approached her with the proper cues and responded appropriately to hers. "He knew exactly what to do, thanks to Blakely."

Blakely and his human caretakers took daily walks through the zoo so that visiting fans could greet him. The walks also gave Blakely a chance to see the animals he has raised, including Dale who runs to the front of his enclosure to greet Blakely with a snort. Blakely recently retired and lives with Strasser and Kuchle, but of the important role the dog has played in the lives of other zoo inhabitants, Strasser says, "I don't know what exactly it is he is doing with them. But I do know that whatever it is, we as humans can't duplicate it. It's about animals talking to each other." And Blakely, it would appear, is fluent in a remarkable number of languages. ◆

BLAKELY HAD NO SPECIAL TRAINING WHEN HE STARTED FOSTERING ZOO ANIMALS. THOUGH INITIALLY WARY, HE WAS SOON OFFERING AROUND-THE-CLOCK CUDDLES TO CHEETAH CUBS (ABOVE), AN OCELOT (LEFT), WALLABIES, AND EVEN A WARTHOG.

SIDEWALK SUPERSTAR: *Louboutina the hugging golden retriever draws a crowd as she doles out hugs to the lucky strangers she meets on the streets of Manhattan.*

# LOUBOUTINA

## AN OPEN ARM POLICY

### Golden retriever •— New York

**W**ho doesn't crave a hug now and then? For those too shy to ask for what we need, there's a dog in New York City's Chelsea neighborhood waiting to welcome you into a warm embrace.

The golden retriever Louboutina first made her penchant for closeness apparent to her owner, Cesar Fernandez-Chavez, when she began insisting on holding his hand at age three. During walks, the dog would sit and continue offering her paw until he would shake it. Soon, she found her balance and would raise her other paw up to put it over his hand holding hers. Then she graduated to placing both paws around his waist. Fernandez-Chavez, who was mourning the end of a long relationship, admits he found it embarrassing to be stopped every 10 steps or so by a dog who insisted on hugging him, but he would jokingly tell friends "At least I have someone to hold hands with before Valentine's Day!"

It turns out that Louboutina isn't picky when it comes to physical contact. When the actor Gerard Butler saw her hugging her owner, he stopped and asked to have a picture taken of the dog hugging him as well. Fernandez-Chavez posted the picture on Instagram, and soon people were flocking to her Manhattan neighborhood to seek her out.

Louboutina has become a star thanks to @louboutinanyc, an Instagram account documenting her natural desire to hug. Fans stand expectantly on corners with their phones and cameras at the ready. One adoring fan went as far as wearing a shirt that she had made that read, "I came to New York to hug Loubie!" Other content themselves by simply falling to their knees before her.

For Fernandez-Chavez, who works in health care, it can be a bit disruptive when he's trying to give the dog a quick run around the block before an appointment; according to him, there isn't a single walk where someone doesn't recognize Louboutina and make a beeline for her. "It can take an hour to walk a whole block," he says, adding that people seem to need her comfort the most during her 5 p.m. walk, which coincides with the end of most work days.

**"PEOPLE WILL CRY OR TALK ABOUT THEIR SITUATIONS, AND THEN THEY HUG HER AND SAY THEY FEEL BETTER."**

"People will cry or talk about their situations, and then they hug her and say they feel better," he says. "And when I am feeling lonely, these stories make me feel like a better person because we are sharing good energy."

No matter how late he may be for a meeting, Fernandez-Chavez says he has yet to deprive anyone of the retriever's embrace. "Hopefully we are a symbol of tolerance and love," he says, adding that he's gotten over the embarrassment of walking with the eccentric dog. "She may be a weirdo," he says. "But she's an angel. She's a weirdo angel." ◆

LOUBOUTINA SITS UP ON HER HAUNCHES TO PLACE BOTH PAWS AROUND PEOPLE'S LEGS (LEFT). IT'S A TRICK SHE LEARNED ON HER OWN, ACCORDING TO HER OWNER, CESAR FERNANDEZ-CHAVEZ (BELOW).

**DUTIFUL DEPUTY:** *Seen here with her partner, Deputy Bullinger, receiving an award, Libby is not only an accomplished police dog, but also an energetic and affectionate advocate for her job and breed.*

# LIBBY

## A NOSE FOR JUSTICE

### Pit bull — Texas

**D**eputy Jesse Bullinger issues a warning to strangers approaching Libby, his narcotics-sniffing pit bull: If you attempt to pet her, she is guaranteed to jump up and lick your face. Libby's ebullient personality belies her lauded work ethic. In her first two years as a drug-detecting K9 for the Montgomery County Constable, she and Bullinger were responsible for busts leading to more than 70 arrests.

Beloved within her department and praised by the public, Libby has become a local celebrity. When she's not working the streets, she's educating the public about her job and her breed—including an appearance at a Houston Astros game to "throw out" the first pitch (she enthusiastically delivered the ball to the player on the field).

Nothing about her early life suggested that Libby would have the chance to make a difference. Abandoned with her littermates at a Montgomery County shelter, her siblings were subsequently put to sleep. When Libby landed on the euthanasia list, she was rescued by the group Operation Pets Alive!, and the organization's head stepped in to foster her. But placing a pit bull can be hard, and Libby's habit of barking when she gets excited—a shrill noise that Bullinger admits can be off-putting—only added to that challenge. The dog spent close to three years being passed over at adoption events.

Then, at one such event, Libby grabbed the attention of pit bull advocate Debra Guajardo, who recognized that the dog's high energy and endless enthusiasm for playing ball were ideal qualities for a working dog. She got in touch with Brad Croft, founder of Universal K9, a dog training center in San Antonio, Texas. Croft had nearly two decades of experience training elite law enforcement dogs before he expanded his business to rescuing pit bulls and turning them into top police dogs.

While Croft considers pit bulls to be great dogs, his decision to work with the breed is entirely practical: They make up the largest population of dogs in Texas shelters. Croft explains that, as with any breed, there are all kinds of pit bulls out there—most of whom make great pets. But there are also those he describes as having "super, super high drive: dogs who don't want to hurt anybody but just can't stand still. They're the ones who are jumping five feet up in the air in their kennels in the shelter." These are the dogs who potential adopters walk by, the ones being put down. And these are the ones who work best for Croft.

His program costs a fraction of the price of buying and training puppies bred for the task, which can run $10,000 to $15,000—a price prohibitive for most law enforcement bureaus. "I knew all these departments needed dogs that they couldn't afford, and I knew dogs in shelters who were capable of doing the work and who were being put down," explains Croft. "I wanted to save some of those dogs, and then donate them to departments who needed them."

The results of his labor have made him well-known within the K9 community, resulting in more requests for training services than Croft can answer. But Guajardo was so persistent that Croft relented and returned her call, requesting a video of Libby playing with a ball. With the camera on, Guajardo threw a ball into the bushes

AFTER BEING RESCUED FROM A EUTHANASIA LIST, LIBBY WASN'T ADOPTED FOR THREE YEARS DUE TO HER EXCITABLE PERSONALITY. HOWEVER, THAT SAME PERSONALITY IS A BIG FACTOR IN HER SUCCESS–SHE HAS BEEN INVOLVED IN MORE THAN 70 ARRESTS.

at twilight as noisy traffic rushed by. Undistracted, Libby disappeared into the underbrush for several minutes until she emerged victorious, tennis ball in mouth.

Within minutes of seeing the footage, Croft knew Libby had the makings of a great police dog. He asked Guajardo to bring her to his training center in San Antonio, more than three hours away. Skills such as tracking and sniffing for drugs have nothing to do with breed, according to Croft. "The dog either has it or doesn't have it," he says. And Libby's determination and temperament—intelligent, focused even around loud noises, *and* her joyful personality—suggested that she had all the right stuff.

**"ALL THE STARS ALIGNED. IT WAS LIKE WINNING THE LOTTERY."**

Guajardo hoped that Libby could be returned to Montgomery County to work when she was done with her six-to-eight week training, so that she could prove that shelter dogs can be of service within their community. Croft said the chances were slim—he had yet to receive any interest from Montgomery in a pit bull, and he already had a request from North Carolina for a dog. Then, a few weeks into Libby's training, he received a call from Montgomery's Bullinger, who was about to retire his bloodhound and was looking for a new partner. Croft said he would donate his training costs if the department would take Libby. Guajardo chipped in for Bullinger's two-week handling course at Croft's facility and for his hotel room during his stay. Says Croft, "All the stars aligned. It was like winning the lottery."

Within days on the job, Libby made her first bust, finding marijuana and other drugs as well as loaded pistols. It took the detection dog even less time to win the hearts of her human colleagues. "She runs all over the office getting treats from the secretaries," Bullinger says. "And everyone just loves her." Libby even has her own Facebook page, maintained by the department, which showcases her frequent accomplishments.

Libby revels in her job, racing out the door with excitement when Bullinger reaches for her working collar. "If I leave her at home because I have a court date, she gets mad," he says. "She sits at the door waiting for me." But as Libby's retirement date nears, he feels confident she will ultimately settle into a life of leisure. "When she's working, she goes 100 miles an hour. But when she's not working, she's really, really lazy." At home, she is found most often on her back, sleeping with all four legs in the air. "We high-five her when we walk by," says Bullinger. And until recently, she slept with his young daughter, until she got tired of Libby's snoring and hogging the covers.

Libby only underperforms in one role: Despite her occasionally menacing appearance on the job, "She's the worst guard dog ever," Bullinger says with a laugh. "If she can even be bothered to get up when someone is at the door, she's just going to greet them with a kiss." Consider us warned. ◆

**PRACTICE MAKES PERFECT:** *Purin is practicing catching mini soccer balls before they go into the goal. She once caught 11 in one minute, earning a title in the Guinness World Records.*

# PURIN

## A WINNING PUP

### Beagle ⊷ Japan

**I**f she weren't so unbelievably cute, it would be easy to dismiss Purin as a show-off. After all, this beagle has held not one but *three* Guinness World Record titles.

Purin caught the most mini soccer balls in one minute before they went into the goal (she "saved" 11 of them in 2015), and then broke that record the next year by catching 14 balls. In 2017, she broke another record for the fastest 10 meters traveled on a ball by a dog (she balanced on an inflatable ball and crossed the finish line in under 10 seconds). She and her owner also won the record for the most skips by a dog and a person with a single jump rope in one minute.

Purin's owner, Tokyo's Makoto Kumagai, recognized that his beagle had what it took when the eight-week-old puppy learned "paw" and "sit" within a day of his bringing her home. Within a week, Purin had mastered "lie down." What was also clear, says Kumagai, was the dog's character—no funny puppy business here. "I realized she is very cool, calm, and brave. My previous beagle was such a wimp, but Purin is strong-minded."

For the first two years that she lived with Kumagai, Purin was sufficiently amused playing with other dogs. But the puppy gradually lost interest in socializing, and

Kumagai worried she would need exercise and mental stimulation. He decided that he would be her playmate and teach her tricks while they were romping about. He started by asking Purin to help him carry a bag. She mastered that task so quickly that he began to teach her more elaborate tricks during their daily 15 minutes of training. Her achievements caught the eye of local scouts from the Guinness World Records, who challenged the duo to try to set some records using Purin's impressive talents.

Like many beagles, Purin is highly food motivated, which means rewarding her behavior is as easy as tossing her a treat. It's no surprise that her favorite activities are eating and sleeping; rest is essential, apparently, for greeting her fans. She's frequently recognized when she's riding her skateboard along Tokyo's streets, a favored mode of transportation thanks to her owner's coaching. Is there anything at which Purin *doesn't* excel? "Nothing rings a bell," says Kumagai. "She's good at everything she does." ◆

PURIN'S OWNER, MAKOTO KUMAGAI (BELOW), REALIZED EARLY ON IN HER TRAINING THAT SHE WAS A TALENTED PUP, SO HE STARTED TEACHING HER TRICKS LIKE BALANCING ON A BALL IN THE PARK (LEFT).

PATIENT PUP: *Izzy is waiting outside of the break room in the Brookdale Kingston senior community where she lives. The other residents love to spoil her with treats and affection.*

# IZZY

## A MODEL (SENIOR) CITIZEN

### Shepherd mix • Tennessee

Izzy has glaucoma, she is hard of hearing, and some mornings she struggles to stand up. In other words, jokes Harold Underwood, one of her many companions at the senior living community Brookdale Kingston, "She fits right in."

The mature shepherd mix arrived at the Kingston, Tennessee, home with her owner and quickly charmed residents and staff. She isn't scared of wheelchairs, never jumps or barks, and she is democratic about letting everyone pet her. So when her owner passed away and no family member could take her, the staff made the dog a permanent resident.

Izzy had slept in the office of the sales and marketing manager, Lesa Fuller, during her owner's hospitalizations, and she still wanders in for catnaps. Another favorite spot is a dog bed in the lobby, where she spends days greeting visitors at the door. Her ever-growing group of devotees includes members of the town who have heard about the four-legged sweetheart and stop by with toys and food. "If there's a complication to having her, we don't know what it is," says Fuller. "She's just perfect."

Underwood admits the dog's only flaw is entirely their fault: "We give her too many treats so she's gotten a little overweight, just like the rest of us. But she's happy, and we're happy." ◆

HUNGRY HEART: *When Hooch was a puppy, he suffered severe abuse that left him unable to eat or drink. Now he is healthy again and works hard spreading happiness as a therapy dog for children.*

# HOOCH

## A SECOND CHANCE

### French mastiff mix •—• California

ooch is the patron dog of the misunderstood. At the Bakersfield, California, shelter where he was staying, the French mastiff mix alarmed workers by throwing his food and water bowls across his kennel. And with ears raw from having been recently clipped, the emaciated dog's looks were as off-putting as his seemingly aggressive behavior.

When Hooch contracted viral pneumonia, the shelter called Zach Skow, founder of Marley's Mutts Dog Rescue, an organization known for handling difficult canines. Skow rushed Hooch to the veterinarian, who immediately intubated the dog to relieve his labored breathing. That's when they saw that Hooch's tongue had been cut out, a discovery that immediately explained his distressing behavior and his thin frame: The dog had been unable to eat or drink.

The veterinarians quickly inserted a feeding tube, but Hooch ripped it out. Determined, Skow never doubted that he and the dog would figure it out. He bought Hooch a Bailey's chair—essentially a child's high chair—that allowed him to drop moistened food to the back of the dog's mouth, which made it easy for Hooch to swallow it. Soon, the dog learned how to drink by sticking his whole face in a water bowl. "It's messy, but it gets the job done," says Skow.

Long before Hooch was released from the hospital, Skow decided that he would adopt the dog himself. A recovering drug addict and alcoholic, Skow had found his way out of a suicidal period by starting Marley's Mutts, a rescue program that focuses its efforts on helping dogs that might not otherwise get a second chance. Marley's Mutts also runs a program that pairs these animals with incarcerated men, who then train them to become therapy dogs. Skow trains the rest of the rescued dogs himself before placing them in adoptive homes.

Understanding Hooch's trauma, Skow sensed that the dog would do well working with children. His intuition was not only correct, but life-changing for Hooch and the many people whom his presence has affected. Hooch earned an American Humane Hero Dog Award for his work as a therapy dog with abused, special needs, and autistic children. Now weighing in at a healthy 92 pounds, the affectionate dog lies on his back awaiting belly rubs and allows himself to be laid on—and, if ignored, he will paw people asking to be petted. Laughs Skow, "It doesn't take a long time for him to warm up." Skow is careful to monitor the amount of time Hooch spends working. The dog can become overwhelmed by crowds and withdraw because of his difficult history. In addition, his inability to pant means that the California summer heat can be punishing if he's not near air conditioning.

But it's his rough start and recovery that make Hooch an inspiration. "When you know what he's been through, you can't help but want to shine yourself," Skow says. His handler knows the dog hasn't forgotten that he was abused, and that he will always have moments of fear. And yet, Skow marvels, "He gets through it. He kisses the dragon on the nose." ◆

HOOCH AND HIS HANDLER, ZACH SKOW (BELOW), POSE IN FRONT OF THE MARLEY'S MUTTS VAN. THE ORGANIZATION HELPS ANIMALS GET A SECOND CHANCE. WITHOUT IT, HOOCH MAY NEVER HAVE BEEN ABLE TO LIVE A FULL LIFE OF FRIENDSHIP AND BELLY RUBS.

CALMING CUDDLES: *Karma, seen here being held by a patient at her owner's dental practice, is brought into appointments to calm patients' anxieties about going to the dentist.*

# KARMA

## A SMILE AT THE READY

### Papillon mix ⊷ California

For a select few, going to the dentist is actually fun—at least for those lucky enough to visit the practice of Cameron Garrett and his dental hygienist wife, Debra. At the Garretts' office in Corte Madera, California, people who experience anxiety during dental appointments can find some relief by holding the couple's senior papillon mix, Karma, who often falls asleep on patients' laps for the duration of procedures.

"The majority of people who are phobic do really well holding her," reports Debra. "And all the others say that not only does she make it so much better, but they actually look forward to coming in."

After the heartbreaking loss of their two dogs, the Garretts had no plans for adopting again. "We just couldn't face it," Debra explains. But she was willing to adopt on behalf of her mother who was suffering from Alzheimer's disease and asking for a dog to keep her company.

Knowing that a small, older dog would be the best match, Debra adopted Karma from Muttville Senior Rescue Dogs in San Francisco. But within two days, it became clear that her mother, who lived nearby, was unable to care for the pet. The Garretts prepared to return Karma to the rescue organization, but in the meantime they brought her to stay at their home. After a few nights of Karma sleeping next to her, Debra was in love. When she took Karma to a planned adoption event, Debra high-tailed it home after one look at the crowd of canines. She explained to her reluctant husband that with so many dogs waiting for homes, Karma's chances of finding a placement were slim. Cameron relented and let Debra keep her.

Karma—who has subsequently had to have all of her teeth removed due to infection—began accompanying the couple to the office. At first, they kept the dog secluded and away from the patients in case her presence was an annoyance. Then people began holding her in the waiting room, and Debra had a thought: Carrying Karma into the treatment room might help soothe nervous patients. The first time Karma sat through an appointment, Debra remembers that the patient questioned if the pet could actually calm her doctor's-office jitters. As soon as the papillon mix settled onto her lap, the patient relaxed. Now Karma's canine support is a planned offering for anyone who wants to be soothed in the patient chair.

Debra says that Karma's job as a lapdog comes naturally—she also provides her signature comfort at home, where she lies curled up beside Debra or her husband. The once reluctant Dr. Garrett has also become besotted with the dog; at the end of a long day, Karma can be found asleep, tucked up under his chin. ◆

WHETHER GOING ON A HIKE IN HER DOGGIE BACKPACK (LEFT), OR CALMING PATIENTS WITH HER PRESENCE IN THE OFFICE (BELOW), IT'S SAFE TO SAY THE ONCE RELUCTANT DR. GARRETT HAS DEVELOPED A SWEET TOOTH FOR KARMA'S COMPANY.

**BEST OF FRIENDS:** *Haley Inness and her service dog, Rosco, go shopping at the Lincoln Children's Museum after touring the exhibits—just one of the many activities they love to do together.*

# ROSCO

## A CONSTANT COMPANION

### Labrador retriever •—• Nebraska

I t was supposed to be a simple Saturday outing to the museum. But while Jennifer Inness and her four year old daughter Haley wandered through the Lincoln Children's Museum in Lincoln, Nebraska, they came upon a group of dogs touring the museum as well.

The canines turned out to be trained service dogs who were part of a presentation given by Domesti-PUPS, a local organization that trains therapy and service dogs for persons with disabilities. That evening, the Inness family spoke about the potential benefits of such a dog for Haley, whose cerebral palsy affects her muscle tone and motor skills and, as a result, requires her to use a wheelchair and a walker. With Haley's doctor's approval, the family joined a two-year waiting list for a Domesti-PUPS pet, the majority of which are rescued. The organization extends its positive impact by teaching inmates at both the Lincoln Correctional Center and Nebraska State Penitentiary to train the dogs, a yearlong commitment that proves therapeutic for both the inmates and the animals.

Inness set about raising the funds for the service dog. The family would need to pitch in $6,000; Domesti-PUPS agreed to cover the remainder of the $24,000 tab with a scholarship. "I had just had a baby, so I was pushing a wheelchair with one hand and a stroller with the other as we pounded the pavement," Inness remembers. "But I was a mom on a mission."

Inness found a church that was willing to host a charity event, and Domesti-PUPS brought dogs to demonstrate their talents: opening doors, bracing people who have trouble standing, and other helpful tricks. The Innesses raised more than their goal and gave the full amount to Domesti-PUPS, and the donations kept coming. Complete strangers pitched in, including a couple who gave $1,000 to pay for a year's worth of dog food and toys for the yet-to-be-appointed support pet. Three months after the fund-raiser, the Innesses received a call: It was time for Haley to attend the 10-day camp where she would learn to work with a service dog specially trained for her needs.

From the first day of camp, Haley hoped she would be paired with a large brown lab named Rosco. His obsession with playing fetch had clued Domesti-PUPS into his potential for training and working when they rescued him, and the instinct would prove to be spot-on. On the last day of camp, Haley attended "graduation" during which the inmate who had spent 18 months training Rosco handed the leash over to his new, petite handler. "It was a very bittersweet moment," says Inness, who still cries at the memory of watching the ceremony. "Here are these inmates who have lived with and trained the dogs for so long and given back to society, and the kids are just looking at them like they're heroes."

What the Innesses couldn't have guessed at the time was that Rosco's trainer would become a part of their lives, too. After he was released from prison, Domesti-PUPS hired him as a staff handler, and he has helped train Rosco when the dog's service skills need a tune-up or as Haley's needs change.

No matter how the dog's duties evolve, the bond between him and Haley remains steadfast. Within a week of Rosco's arrival, Haley needed a new bed—the two couldn't fit in her twin bed and they refused to sleep apart. At night, Rosco pulls

WHETHER EXPLORING MUSEUMS (LEFT) OR RIDING IN FIRE TRUCKS (BELOW), IT IS HARD TO FIND A TIME WHEN ROSCO AND HALEY AREN'T ADVENTURING. HE'S HELPED HER ACHIEVE A LEVEL OF INDEPENDENCE THAT WASN'T PREVIOUSLY POSSIBLE.

SHE MARVELS AT THE EASE
OF THEIR RELATIONSHIP.
"YOU KNOW HOW IN A MARRIAGE
PEOPLE FINISH EACH OTHER'S
SENTENCES?" INNESS ASKS.
"THAT'S HOW THEY ARE TOGETHER."
WITHOUT EVER A CROSS WORD.

the blankets up to Haley's hands so that she can grab them and tuck them in around herself; in the morning, he wakes her up with kisses. "I think it's the grossest thing," Inness says with a laugh. "He licks her hands, her feet, and her face but she just giggles. They both love it so much."

Rosco braces Haley as she gets in or out of her wheelchair, climbs into bed, or maneuvers through the bathroom—things that once required the assistance of an adult. The loving lab also opens doors and refrigerators for her, and—what is Haley's favorite trick—he will bring her a package of crackers and a bottle of water if she's playing in the basement. But it's the emotional rewards of companionship that have meant the most to Haley. "Before I got Rosco I was very shy," she says. "And he has opened me up to things I didn't even know existed. I have so much more confidence with him around."

He's seldom *not* around. If Haley chooses to go somewhere without him, the devoted dog sits by the door and waits for her return. When friends come over, "He doesn't like to share me," Haley says. His adorable and relentless attention-stealing tactic is to shower her with stuffed animals.

Inness acknowledges that having a service dog has its challenges. It is difficult to care for another creature's demands in addition to her two children and the family dog, a lab mix. And it is an ongoing commitment to make sure Haley and Rosco stay disciplined in their partnership so that Rosco can meet her changing needs as she gets older. But the mother weeps with gratitude when she talks about how Rosco has changed all of their lives, and she marvels at the ease of their relationship. "You know how in a marriage people finish each other's sentences?" Inness asks. "That's how they are together." Without ever a cross word. ◆

SUPER SNIFFER: *Angus, seen here with his owner and trainer, Teresa Zurberg, was a bomb-detection dog who made a career change; now he detects a life-threatening bacteria called* C. diff.

# ANGUS

## SNIFFING OUT A SUPERBUG

**English springer spaniel ⊷ Vancouver, Canada**

Teresa Zurberg trained bomb- and drug-detection dogs before an injury led to a new opportunity working with talented canines. While being treated for a gash on her leg at a local hospital in 2013, Zurberg caught *Clostridium difficile*, or *C. diff*, a potentially lethal superbug that is estimated to infect upward of half a million people in the U.S. each year. The bug is becoming increasingly severe, costly, and difficult to treat. Zurberg recovered, but hoping to save others from the same ordeal, her husband—a nurse at the hospital—suggested that her working dog, Angus, trade sniffing bombs for bacteria.

Vancouver General Hospital's infectious disease department agreed to pilot a program with Zurberg and the springer spaniel. Encouraged by a reward of playing with his favorite toy, a purple squeaky hippo, Angus was trained to detect specimens of *C. diff*, which are invisible to the human eye. Then Zurberg began taking him to the hospital to acquaint him with wheelchairs, high-pitched noises from machines, and what she calls "general chaos." Within months, Angus—with Zurberg by his side—was a full-time hospital employee.

The pair begin their hospital patrol at 6 a.m. each day. When Angus locates a bacterial threat, cleaning crews come and disinfect the area before the dog and handler move on. With a 97 percent rate of accuracy, Angus has become a literal poster child in the hospital—his image adorns a billboard at the entrance—but the springer spaniel is largely appreciated from afar. As a working dog, the staff and visitors are asked not to pet him, a request that is largely respected. "It can get a little crazy when there is a group of nursing students," Zurberg says. "But when he's working, his focus needs to stay on me." Still, the popular pooch gets plenty of affection: He has trained Zurberg's officemate to give him regular belly rubs during his breaks.

At home, Angus plays with his canine siblings—fellow rescues Dodger and Captain Cupcake—and demands to play fetch day and night. He also has a play pool in which he swims, although he is on his second, sturdier model after destroying the first in short order. Thanks to her energetic companions, Zurberg admits to being a bit sleep deprived: "Angus doesn't have an off switch, but he's so cute and he uses that against me on a regular basis." The first *C. diff* detection dog will soon have some competition: Zurberg is training Dodger to alert to the bacteria as hospitals are clamoring for their own lifesaving poster boy. ◆

ANGUS IS A CERTIFIED VOLUNTEER OF THE VANCOUVER GENERAL HOSPITAL (LEFT). WHEN HE ISN'T ACTIVELY SEARCHING FOR *C. DIFF* BACTERIA, HE CAN BE FOUND DOING DEMONSTRATIONS SO THE PROGRAM CAN EXPAND TO OTHER HOSPITALS (BELOW).

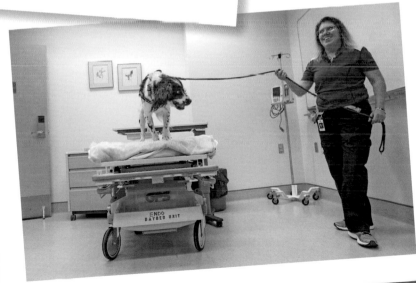

LEADING LADY: *Good-looking Freya graced the silver screen in* Transformers: The Last Knight. *Director Michael Bay cast the pooch in an effort to destigmatize pit bulls as a "bully breed."*

# FINALLY AT HOME

## Pit bull ⊶ Mobberley, England

**D**espite spending six years at the Freshfields Animal Rescue, Freya was far from being "the world's loneliest dog," as the media would famously dub her. In fact, the pit bull was a favorite at the shelter, frequently going home with staff members for some extra love to keep her spirits up as she remained while other dogs came and went.

Freya had arrived at the shelter as a stray in 2010, and her exuberant personality quickly won her fans. Yet, of an estimated 18,000 people who visited the shelter during Freya's stay, not one expressed an ongoing interest in adopting her. "Freya came to us when a lot of people no longer liked the breed," says head of kennels Collette Piert, who says Freya is one of her favorite residents ever. Piert, who would spend weekends taking Freya on hikes along with her own dogs, attributes the public mindset partly to negative media coverage of pit bulls. And Freya's shelter upbringing also meant that her manners could use work.

When Freya turned six, she began experiencing epileptic seizures. In an attempt to draw attention to the dog and secure a home where she could receive full-time care, a journalist wrote an article calling her "the loneliest dog in the world." Among the readers of the piece was film director Michael Bay, who quickly decided to act

THE COUPLE HAD SPENT YEARS
CARING FOR AND ADOPTING RESCUE
DOGS, AND FREYA RESEMBLED ONE
OF THEIR BELOVED PETS WHO
HAD RECENTLY DIED FROM CANCER,
A LOSS THAT HAD DEVASTATED THEM.
JACKIE SUGGESTED VISITING
THE SHELTER TO MEET FREYA.
ACCORDING TO RAY, "IT WAS FATE."

and was determined to give people a positive view of the breed. He cast Freya in his 2017 movie *Transformers: The Last Knight* and took to social media to say that if no one adopted the dog after her cinematic debut, she would live with him. The media seized on the story.

One morning, the sudden canine star was the guest on a talk show that Jackie Collins happened to be watching, and she immediately alerted her husband, Ray. The couple from Mobberley—a village about half an hour from Freshfields Animal Rescue—had spent years caring for and adopting rescue dogs, and Freya resembled one of their beloved pets who had recently died from cancer, a loss that had devastated them. Jackie suggested visiting the shelter to meet Freya. According to Ray, "It was fate."

By then offers to adopt the celebrity pit bull were coming in from all over the world. But Piert and her colleagues wanted to keep Freya close to the shelter so that she could always return to a familiar environment should a family change their minds once they had taken her home. When the Collinses reached out, there were initial concerns about bringing Freya into the family's mix of other pets, but Piert remembers, "I somehow just felt like these were people who could make it work."

At their first meeting, "Freya ran at me and humped me and bit both my arms," Collins recalls good-naturedly. The shelter staff apologized and said, "We'll understand if you walk away, but otherwise come back next week." The Collinses returned the following week—the first family ever to follow up with Freya after an initial visit—and they continued showing up for seven weeks after that. Soon enough the Collinses were granted overnight visits with Freya at their home, and finally they were allowed to adopt her. An additional prize: They were able to visit the film set while Freya had her moment of fame and earned the accolades of the actor Anthony Hopkins, who snuggled up to the dog for a photo.

Collins admits that Freya isn't the world's easiest dog to handle, but his experience with a tough range of pets puts him up to the challenge. She still has seizures even while on her epilepsy medication, and an episode can leave her disoriented for a couple of hours. But now that she is settled in a permanent home, fun-loving Freya has calmed down and is friendly with people. By day, she's an ideal companion: She accompanies Collins to work where he is a car salesman, and the two stop by the usual pet stores to collect treats; she even joins her owners at the pub for a pint. Collins stays with her through it all. "She's a handful," he says. "But she's a lovely handful."

## "SHE'S A HANDFUL," HE SAYS. "BUT SHE'S A LOVELY HANDFUL."

Freya's legacy is connecting the people who have dedicated themselves to caring for her: the Collinses frequently send photos and updates to those who tended to her at Freshfields, and they host a Christmas gathering where they all reunite to toast a happy girl who finally has a home of her own. Says Piert, "It's something that I wished for her for so long." As it has turns out, Freya's long wait for a family landed her more than just one. ◆

WHY DOESN'T ANYONE WANT ME?

I'VE BEEN WAITING HERE FOR 5 YEARS + 2 MONTHS NOW → WHICH IS A TOTAL OF 1889 DAYS!

PEOPLE HAVE BEEN TO MEET ME, BUT THEY NEVER COME BACK FOR ME? I KNOW THAT I CAN BE A HANDFUL AT FIRST BUT IT IS ONLY BECAUSE I GET SO EXCITED.

I PROMISE I WILL BE A GOOD GIRL WHEN I SETTLE IN. I HAVE NEVER HAD MY OWN FAMILY, MAYBE YOU COULD BE MY FAMILY?

I SIT AND WAIT FOR YOU TO COME...

🐾 FREYA

FREYA WAS PASSED OVER BY ADOPTING FAMILIES FOR MORE THAN FIVE YEARS (ABOVE). AMONG HER SYMPATHIZERS WAS DIRECTOR MICHAEL BAY, WHO CAST FREYA IN A MOVIE OPPOSITE ACTOR ANTHONY HOPKINS (LEFT) TO RAISE AWARENESS OF HER STORY.

PRODUCTIVE PALS: *K9 Gia and her handler, Joni Zimmermann, are more than just partners; they're best friends. Feeding off of each other's success makes them one of the most productive teams around.*

# GIA

## ON THE PATH OF JUSTICE

### Shepherd mix •— Florida

**D**etective Joni Zimmermann had never worked with a dog trained in electronic detection, nor did her department have the funds for such a canine. But when her sergeant returned from a 2015 conference raving about the work of a Labrador retriever detection dog who was able to sniff out electronic data devices that are small and easily hidden, Zimmermann knew that a four-legged employee was what her team needed.

Zimmermann was used to frustrating and even heartbreaking days at the Child Protection Specialist Unit in the sheriff's department of Manatee County, where she tracked child predators. A dog who could find devices that contained illegal content could help convict criminals, but at the time, there were just five dogs in the country with this particular ability. Nevertheless, Zimmermann was committed to finding a canine to train, and she committed to being the dog's handler.

She started by contacting Lieutenant Dennis Cunningham, who was in charge of training the K9s for the sheriff's department. It was the right call: Cunningham had spent years preparing expensive patrol and detection dogs to join law enforcement teams, and he spent his personal time volunteering at local shelters. He was confident that when it came to odor detection, he could train a rescue dog for the task.

The lieutenant takes an alternative approach to training, believing that the most important trait isn't a genetically gifted nose or drive, but rather, an attachment to his or her handler. "If the dog wants to please his or her person," Cunningham explains. "That's all the reward they need."

Zimmermann and Cunningham began visiting shelters, but the standard choices—Labrador retrievers who had failed out of guide dog programs for their hyperactivity, which can belie an excellent work ability—didn't fit the bill. The reason, says Cunningham, had nothing to do with the dogs. It was a lack of something between the dogs and Zimmermann. The trainer was looking for an interaction that he couldn't put into words, but that he knew he would recognize instantly—the makings of an unbreakable bond.

Finally, at a shelter where Cunningham is a financial donor, the search ended with Gia. At six months, the shepherd mix was half a year younger than Cunningham's usual charges, but he spotted that special connection he had been looking for between Zimmermann and the dog. "I fell in love with her the minute they brought her into the room," Zimmermann remembers. "I wanted her to be the one." But they would need the department's official permission to adopt her, so the detective said a painful goodbye to her new friend for that day.

Unknown to Zimmermann, Cunningham returned to the office and made a strong case to the sheriff. "I explained their connection would be the overall factor in the success of the program," Cunningham remembers. Two days later, the request to bring Gia into the department was approved, and the detective returned to get her dog.

For the first few weeks, Zimmermann and Gia's "job" was to become best friends. Gia accompanied her new master everywhere, from the workplace to stores to movies, and it didn't take long for the attachment to form. And once Zimmermann earned the dog's love, her loyalty and willingness to please came with it. Next came the obedience work, followed by the scent training. Gia would be shown a towel she considered a toy, and then Zimmermann would hide the towel with a hard drive wrapped inside and ask her to find it. Eventually, the towel was removed from the process, and Gia was finding electronic devices with no other scents as hints.

On the third day of Gia's training, Cunningham hid a thumb drive under a garbage can without telling Zimmermann, and then led everyone out for a walk. Gia veered toward the garbage can. Cunningham was astonished: "I took a video of it that I wish everyone could see. But I used a bad word in it—I was so shocked," he says with a laugh. The trainer hadn't yet taught Gia how to alert, but the ace canine was scratching at the hidden drive and whining to call attention to it. Three weeks later, Cunningham hid a disc drive in the office of the state attorney as a demonstration; Gia found it within minutes.

Cunningham, who believes that dogs' intelligence is greater than anyone gives them credit for, says that of all the teams he's trained, he's most proud of his work with Gia and Zimmermann. The duo is a living, working example of his theory that the bond is all that matters. "Dogs mimic who their owner is," Cunningham explains. "When she locates a hide, Gia is far more excited about Zimmermann being happy than the reward. They literally feed off of each other on an emotional level."

**"THIS WORK IS SO HARD, AND SO STRESSFUL. AND SHE BRINGS JOY TO US ALL."**

For the department—and the surrounding community—Gia is a gift who locates key evidence that humans have overlooked. The skilled tracker has assisted the team in finding disc drives in the homes of suspects in child predator cases, helping to put away criminals and keep local areas safer. More than that, Gia's simple presence is a comfort to the entire unit. "This work is so hard, and so stressful," says Zimmermann. "And she brings joy to us all." ◆

COURTROOM COMFORT: *Karl, a deaf boxer therapy dog, provides emotional support to children asked to give testimony in court.*

# KARL

## THE BEST LISTENER

### Boxer 🦴 Florida

Here's to connections. Karl was three weeks old when his breeder reached out to Joanne Hart-Rittenhouse. Hart-Rittenhouse, a well-known fixture within the southeast boxer rescue community, was told that Karl was deaf, and unless the breeder could find a good home for him, she was going to euthanize him. Hart-Rittenhouse, who lives in Orlando, immediately said she would help.

Then she called a friend in a panic: What was she going to do with a deaf puppy? Her friend reminded her that she was already taking her other three rescued boxers to a local academy for deaf children as visiting therapy dogs. Why not add Karl to the visits and have him learn American Sign Language (ASL) and other signed commands? Hart-Rittenhouse immediately began training him, and now, the former student is acting as the teacher: Karl, who quickly mastered more than 120 signs, helps others learn sign language by allowing them to practice words such as "friends," "I love you," and "cookie" (he loves cookies). "He's so excited when someone [can] communicate with him," says Hart-Rittenhouse.

When Karl turned one, Hart-Rittenhouse took him to be registered as a therapy dog. He struggled only with the part of the test that required going into a nursing home because the scent overwhelmed his extra-sensitive nose. "It didn't smell good, and he wanted no part of it," Hart-Rittenhouse remembers. "But I just kept signing to him that everyone was friends. According to Karl, everyone in the world is his friend." And with the incentive of meeting more pals, the boxer passed the test.

Now that friendly attitude is one for which scores of young children are grateful. Karl's therapy-dog calling has turned out to be as a companion to children in courthouses who are asked to give testimony that might be harrowing for them. In addition to his kindness, Karl's size can be a plus. "There was a little girl who had to testify against someone and she said, 'Will Karl protect me if he tries to get me?'" remembers Hart-Rittenhouse. The boxer's imposing presence is empowering. Karl, who remains in the children's lives as long as they wish to visit him, is also a source of comfort to his owner. "Some of the testimony is so awful I just want to cry, but I don't fall apart until I get in the car and I can hug him."

On off days, Karl rotates with his rescue-turned-therapy-dog siblings on visits to imprisoned young people to help with teaching humane treatment of animals.

Working with a deaf dog has its complications, Hart-Rittenhouse acknowledges. While a hearing puppy learns that his or her behavior in the pack is too rough through auditory cues from littermates, a deaf puppy needs to learn to look for a "too rough" sign from humans. But the upsides of a deaf dog, says Hart-Rittenhouse, who has since rescued another deaf boxer, make them her favorite pets. "They sleep well, they don't bark, and they're not scared of thunder or lightning." The only caveat, she admits, is that with their intelligence, they learn quickly that if they refuse to look at her, they don't have to "listen." ◆

"[DEAF DOGS] SLEEP WELL, THEY DON'T BARK, AND THEY'RE NOT SCARED OF THUNDER OR LIGHTNING." THE ONLY CAVEAT, SHE ADMITS, IS THAT WITH THEIR INTELLIGENCE, THEY LEARN QUICKLY THAT IF THEY REFUSE TO LOOK AT HER, THEY DON'T HAVE TO "LISTEN."

JUSTICE IN JERSEY: *Ben Shore and his service dog, Charlie, helped to make New Jersey laws more accepting of service dogs. Now, service dogs cannot be refused entry to a public place without cause.*

# CHARLIE

## A CASE FOR COMPANIONSHIP

### Poodle–golden retriever ⊷ New Jersey

Charlie was just going to be Ben Shore's pet. But he aced both basic and advanced obedience classes when he was only a few months old. Then, without any training, Charlie began to alert to Ben's anxiety attacks, leaning in to his owner to signal an oncoming episode.

Working with a professional, the family trained Charlie to sound the alarm by barking instead. "He gets it maybe 10 minutes before I know [an episode] is going to happen," says Shore, a 15-year-old on the autism spectrum. "I can get out of the situation, and it's all good."

As a certified service dog, Charlie should have been able to accompany Ben everywhere. But Ben's school had a policy denying dogs access to the grounds. The Shore family disputed the ban by introducing a bill to the New Jersey Legislature that would fine anyone who refused to allow a service canine into a public place without cause. Months later, the state passed Charlie's Law, so named for the exemplary dog.

Ben now goes days without anxiety attacks. As for Charlie, offering calm doesn't seem stressful. Says Ben, "In math class, he just goes to sleep on my foot. [It is his way of saying,] 'I hate math; this is so boring.'" Luckily for Charlie, unlike his owner, he doesn't have to pay attention. ◆

ALL ABOUT THE CHASE: *Most dogs are afraid of thunderstorms, but not Joplin. Here, her storm-chasing owner snapped a picture as she posed with an EF-3 tornado near Dodge City, Kansas.*

# JOPLIN

## STORM CHASER

### Jack Russell–English pointer mix •—• Texas

Joplin shares her name with the city in Missouri where a tornado hit in 2011. The geographical Joplin was dubbed the City of Hope after the disaster, reflecting the tenacity of its residents that photographer Mike Mezeul II witnessed firsthand.

A veteran storm chaser, Mezeul had flown to Missouri to photograph the tornadoes. When he saw the destruction they had caused, he decided to extend his stay and support the recovery effort. After that experience, Mezeul knew how to recognize resilience when he saw it—even in canine form.

That spirit is exactly what came to mind when Mezeul later adopted a young pup from a Texas shelter. Within hours of bringing her home, the dog was showing signs of parvovirus, which can be lethal for canines. Mezeul's previous dog had also suffered from parvo, so he knew the signs: lethargy, diarrhea, vomiting, and a lack of interest in food and water. Mezeul and his then-girlfriend immediately rushed the yet-to-be-named Joplin to the vet, who started an IV to keep her hydrated (there is no medication to treat the virus). On the fifth day, the couple was told to prepare for the worst. "She was a skeleton," Mezeul remembers. But after two weeks of treatment, Joplin miraculously pulled through.

As Mezeul resumed storm chasing from his home base outside of Dallas, Joplin started experiencing terrible separation anxiety from being boarded at the vet's office while Mezeul was gone. "The vet said, 'She's going to have a heart attack if she stays here,'" Mezeul explains. He thought about giving up the chase to stay home with Joplin, but instead decided to invite her along for the ride. "She loves being in the car, so I said, 'Hop in!'"

Soon, the pair was making history, as the photographer chronicled the dog's adventures playing fetch with a piece of hail, or watching thunder and lightning in Texas's tornado alley. "She's my kid and partner in crime," says Mezeul. He began posting the series of photographs, which he titled "Dog Days of Chasing," to his website, and Joplin rapidly became an online star. For the lucky storm chasers who have met her in person, the playful canine is considered good luck.

It turns out that Joplin is that rare dog who loves storms. At home, one of Joplin's favorite ways to pass the time is sitting on the porch and watching lightning. And "If I say, 'Do you want to go chasing?' she'll fly out the door," says Mezeul. She's now seen more than a dozen tornadoes and been in winds of up to 90 mph while out on the road. He admits that there are inevitably times when conditions scare him, yet Joplin is always unwaveringly calm. "She never gets nervous," he says with wonder. "We've been in a couple of hairy situations where I'm trying not to freak out wondering if we would make it out, and she looks at me like, How's it going?" A storm may look like miserable weather to most, but this fearless and resilient dog is in her element. ◆

WHILE CHASING A STORM, PHOTOGRAPHER MIKE MEZEUL AND JOPLIN WILL OFTEN WAIT FOR A SUPERCELL THUNDER-STORM TO COME TOGETHER (BELOW). JOPLIN'S FAVORITE SPOT TO WATCH? THE HOOD OF THE CAR, TAKING IN THE SIGHTS AND SMELLS (LEFT).

LOVE AND VALOR: *Veteran Jason Haag and his service dog, Axel, pictured waiting for a train, are close companions whose mutual need most likely saved both of their lives.*

# AXEL

## A MISSION TO HEAL

**German shepherd ⋙ Virginia**

P urple Heart recipient and retired Marine Corps Capt. Jason Haag served three tours of duty in Iraq and Afghanistan. He incurred PTSD on his first combat deployment in 2003, and the condition steadily worsened; by the time he returned to his home in Virginia in 2011, he was suffering from a traumatic brain injury as well as anxiety, flashbacks, rage, and a debilitating depression that no medication or therapy seemed to help.

Haag spent the majority of his time in the basement of the house he shared with his wife and three children. After 18 months of Haag isolating himself from his family, his wife gave him an ultimatum: Start making different decisions or lose his family.

Addicted to alcohol and pain medication, Haag says he felt helpless. But some unexplained feeling prompted him to Google service dogs on the Internet. His online search yielded information on four organizations in the business of training dogs for those in need. The first never responded to Haag's inquiry about adopting a pet. The second and third organizations answered with the standard response: He would have to wait at least two years for a trained companion. The fourth organization, K9s For Warriors, based in Florida, responded that they could get him a trained dog in eight months. Haag agreed.

K9s For Warriors had rescued Axel, a German shepherd, from euthanasia when he was nine months old. Now it was the puppy's turn to do the rescuing. Trainers taught the dog to recognize and respond to the signals of a pending anxiety attack or nightmare: Hand wringing or foot tapping usually meant a panic attack was imminent, in which case Axel could lick his handler's face to bring him back to the moment. Thrashing in bed meant that the veteran was experiencing a terrible nightmare, so the dog was taught to gently take a hand in his mouth to prevent Haag from hurting himself.

## "I KNEW THAT WE WERE GOING TO TAKE CARE OF EACH OTHER."

Once the initial training was complete, K9s For Warriors called Haag to their campus to meet his new companion. At the time, his anxiety was still so high that he couldn't manage the airport crowds, so he chartered a private plane to Ponte Vedra Beach, Florida, where he would spend 19 days learning to work with Axel.

The former marine professed that he was not a dog person and recalls, "It was not love at first sight." But the meeting portended positive things to come: "I felt hope, a sense of shared mutual respect," Haag explains. "I knew that we were going to take care of each other." When Haag and Axel landed back in Virginia, the pair went directly to Haag's son's baseball game—the first one Haag had been able to attend in two years.

Four months later, Haag and Axel traveled to Colorado to participate in a snowboarding rehabilitation program for wounded veterans. The two were sitting in the hotel when Haag caught Axel raising an eyebrow. Haag says there was something

AXEL WAS RESCUED BY K9S FOR WARRIORS, AN ORGANIZATION THAT TRAINED HIM TO MEET JASON HAAG'S NEEDS. THE TWO WON THE SERVICE DOG CATEGORY AT THE AMERICAN HUMANE'S FIFTH ANNUAL HERO DOG AWARDS IN 2015 (LEFT).

HAAG IS NOW CEO OF LEASHES OF VALOR, AN ORGANIZATION THAT PAIRS VETERANS WITH SHELTER DOGS BOUND FOR EUTHANASIA. HE RECENTLY PARTICIPATED IN A&E'S DOGS OF WAR 2K-9 RACE IN WASHINGTON, D.C., (BELOW) WITH FELLOW ADVOCATES LINDSEY AND JIM STANEK.

in that facial expression to prompt him to say, "Dude, we made it. Everything's going to be all right." Since then, he has never thought otherwise.

Haag's 17-year marriage did not survive the haul, although he says that he and his ex-wife remain close friends. "Taking care of someone who is wounded is exceptionally draining," he explains. "And your spouse becomes a nurse." But in Axel, Haag has found a 24-hour caregiver who can be by his side at a moment's notice. The unconditional love between them is something Haag now makes an effort to share with other veterans as a way to combat the epidemic of suicide within his community.

Haag has since spearheaded a new organization, Leashes of Valor, a program that pairs dogs rescued from euthanasia with veterans in need of support. As the CEO, Haag has helped partner more than 200 desperate veterans with dogs. "I want to put a leash in every veteran's hands," says Haag. After his 13-year career in the Marines, "My job now is to save as many dogs and people as I can." ◆

CUTE WITH A CAUSE: *Serving as TurfMutt, Lucky—usually decked out in his cape—and owner Kris Kiser spread the importance of being environmentally conscious to school children.*

# LUCKY

## AN ENVIRONMENTAL SUPERHERO

### Pit bull mix ⋈ Virginia

**N**ot every dog can pull off a tablecloth as a cape, but Lucky does and he wears his for an important mission: To educate millions of children about the environment.

When Kris Kiser spotted an emaciated puppy dodging traffic along a highway, he opened his car door and the dog jumped in. It was the beginning of a close partnership—one in which the dog would rarely leave his owner's side. Lucky, so named because of his fortuitous rescue, would accompany Kiser to his job as president and CEO of the Outdoor Power Equipment Institute, a D.C.-based trade organization that represents the interests of landscaping companies and equipment manufacturers.

Kiser didn't expect his new pet to be anything other than an office companion, but in 2007, the drought in California prompted the Environmental Protection Agency to ask residents to consider ripping up their lawns and non-native grasses and plants to help conserve the water supply. In order to protect landscapes, Kiser saw a need to educate people about how the right plants in the right places could actually encourage conservation. "We have to help pollinators, giving bees, birds, and bats a place to rest," he explains. "We need to talk about the environment, which starts in our backyards."

Kiser approached his company's board with his campaign idea, but it was missing a key component: a spokesperson to deliver the educational message. Kiser remembers being pitched ferrets, birds, and squirrels, but he kept coming back to the idea of a canine. After all, he pointed out, who knows a backyard better? Finally, at a subsequent brainstorming meeting, someone at the table looked down, where Lucky was lying at Kiser's feet, as usual . "Will he wear a cape?" his colleague asked. She pulled the cloth off the table and tied it around his neck. "And there it was," says Kiser. "TurfMutt was born."

The program began with weekly flyers delivered to schools in Sacramento and in D.C. featuring TurfMutt, a superhero "saving the planet one yard at a time." Scholastic, Inc., began including TurfMutt in their educational materials to engage children in backyard science and inspire children to be environmental superheroes as well. Lucky—"the Clark Kent to Superman," as Kiser puts it—was a rapidly rising star.

The talented pet still makes appearances at schools, but Kiser admits that unlike his public persona, Lucky prefers solitude. He has the run of Kiser's home, with designated spots on sofas and chairs as well as dog beds in the closets—some of his favorite hideouts. Lucky has given Kiser a personal lift in addition to all of his professional work: "When I'm feeling bad and have the sheets up pulled over my head, Lucky will keep at me until I'm out of bed and shaking it off."

It's a gift Kiser is determined to repay, whether by teaching children how to help protect the earth or how to aid a less fortunate dog. "Lucky saved my life," Kiser says. "The least we can do is *paw* it forward." ◆

OWNER KISER AND LUCKY (BELOW) PARTICIPATE IN TURFMUTT'S OUTREACH PROGRAMS EVERY YEAR, INCLUDING STUDENT SUSTAINABILITY COMPETITIONS. KASHVI RAMANI (LEFT) RECEIVED THE GRAND PRIZE FOR HER ENTRY—AN ENVIRONMENTAL RAP SONG.

FATED FRIENDS: *Six-year-old Ginger was recovering from cancer when her soon-to-be owner, Jody Patterson, saw her photo. Patterson, also a cancer survivor, immediately knew it was the perfect match.*

# GINGER

## A CANCER SURVIVOR'S
## SOUL MATE

### Shar-pei mix ✦ Ohio

A volunteer at a shelter in Ohio was walking a six-year-old shar-pei mix named Leopard when the dog lay down and refused to move. Leopard appeared fixated on a sewer grate in the road. When the volunteer at last came closer, she heard a faint mewing from within the sewer. The authorities were promptly called and a hapless dehydrated cat was brought to freedom. The dog's simple act had saved the cat's life.

Local news outlets rallied around the story, and the shelter hoped that the publicity would help Leopard get adopted. She had already spent six months at the Cuyahoga County Animal Shelter recovering from cancer when she experienced her unexpected minute of fame. Older than most dogs in the shelter and with a complicated health history, Leopard had a difficult time finding a forever home. While the phones soon began ringing with interested parties, no offers materialized into a suitable home.

Meanwhile in nearby Ashtabula, Jody Patterson, a nurse, was recovering from the grueling treatment of clear-cell carcinoma, a rare form of endometrial cancer.

She was in remission but exhausted and finding it difficult to motivate herself to move around as much as she should. She decided an older dog might offer comfort and be a companion in her healing.

After unsuccessful trips to local shelters, Patterson expanded her search. She had missed media coverage of Leopard's heroic deed, but she stumbled across Leopard's profile online. "I immediately thought, We're a match!" Patterson remembers. "She had had cancer, just like me, and in dog years, we were the same age." Still, Patterson's persistent physical weakness made her hesitant to be responsible for another being.

It took two months of looking at the dog's photograph every day for Patterson to feel ready to meet her. She asked her sister to accompany her to the shelter, where the two sat side-by-side waiting to meet Leopard. When the dog entered the room, she immediately approached Patterson and laid her head on her knee. "She came straight for me," says Patterson. "And that was it." Although she had a lingering moment of anxiety, "I reminded myself: I've raised a child, I can do this."

Patterson, who rechristened the dog Ginger, only learned about her brush with fame as she signed the adoption papers, although she says she wasn't surprised given the dog's caring nature.

Within a month of living together, Patterson went from struggling to walk to the end of her block to taking her ever cheerful friend on a mile-long jaunt. "I want to make her happy," says Patterson. "Before, I was so tired I wouldn't want to go to the store, but now I think, Maybe Ginger would enjoy a car ride."

Ginger is everything Patterson had hoped for when she first stumbled onto the dog's photograph, even if it turns out that these days Ginger would rather chase a cat than save one. Shelter administrator Mindy Naticchioni isn't surprised. Of Ginger's "hero" moment, she says with a laugh, "If she hadn't lain down and alerted, we wouldn't have known the cat was there. But let's be honest. Leopard didn't want to play with the cat. She was a little interested in eating it." ◆

WHEN THE DOG ENTERED
THE ROOM, SHE IMMEDIATELY
APPROACHED PATTERSON AND
LAID HER HEAD ON HER KNEE.
"SHE CAME STRAIGHT
FOR ME," SAYS PATTERSON.
"AND THAT WAS IT."

TWICE THE FUN: *For young Averie Mitchell and Hattie Mae, a three-legged Labrador mix, a chance encounter in the waiting room of a prosthetics clinic was the beginning of a beautiful friendship.*

# HATTIE MAE

## A SENSE OF PLAY

**Labrador mix ●—● Oklahoma**

**A**verie Mitchell lost a leg to a condition affecting her tibia at age two. She now wears a prosthetic that enables her mobility and even allows her to compete as a gymnast. One day, while Averie was at an appointment for a new prosthetic, a dog named Hattie Mae arrived for treatment.

The dog's foster owner hoped that a prosthetic might ease the mobility issues Hattie Mae faced after being rescued from a drug house with a missing foot. When Averie spotted Hattie Mae, she turned to her mother and exclaimed, "She's just like me— she doesn't have a right leg either!" Soon the newfound soul mates were sitting together, with Hattie Mae resting her head in Averie's lap. The Mitchells had no intention of adopting another dog—they were happy with just their mutt, Flower. However, two weeks later, the Mitchells decided that their family had room for one more, and they welcomed Hattie Mae into their home.

Averie and her canine sidekick are inseparable—and unstoppable. They bounce on a trampoline and swim together, as well as play with other children. After Averie's last surgery, she spent a night in the hospital where she met therapy dogs, and she now hopes that Hattie Mae will become one as well. Averie's mother, who never doubts the pair's collective strength and spirit, adds, "They amaze me every day." ◆

BEDSIDE MANNER: *Once burdened by a crippling fear of other dogs, Maui is now an indispensable source of comfort to patients at the Animal Wellness Clinic in Indiana.*

# MAUI

## VETERINARY ASSISTANT

### Lhasa apso 🦴 Indiana

At the Animal Wellness Clinic in Michigan City, Indiana, no dog awakens alone after surgery, thanks to Maui, a petite Lhasa apso, who keeps the animals company from exam room to recovery room. Her canine sister, Maple, an affectionate Great Dane–shepherd mix, is also there to help and can often be found in the waiting room comforting anxious owners.

Maui and Maple's owner, Linda Orlowski-Smith, who works as a veterinary assistant at the clinic, began taking Maui to work immediately after adopting her. Emaciated and terrified, the abused pup had spent her first eight months of life locked in a shed. "She had never seen the light of day, literally," says Orlowski-Smith. "And she didn't know anything about being a dog." Orlowski-Smith hoped that by spending her days at the office with other animals, Maui might learn by observation.

Helping Maui find her confidence took patience. At first, the recovering canine would become so upset when someone tried to put a leash on her that she would vomit; so Orlowski-Smith used a string instead, attaching it to a paper clip that hooked onto Maui's collar. At the office, Maui would sit frozen, paralyzed by fear when other dogs approached. But Orlowski-Smith stayed firm when co-workers suggested she pick her up: The dog, she insisted, needed to figure out how to navigate the world on her own.

A couple of months into Maui's adoption, a Doberman started to hound her, and the little Lhasa apso finally turned around and barked in protest. That simple canine version of "no" was monumental for Maui. "From that moment she knew how to ask to be left alone," remembers Orlowski-Smith. With her newfound sense of confidence, Maui became a natural leader. She guides anxious dogs up to the examining table and stays close throughout their visits. She accompanies them to surgery and lies next to them until they awaken from general anesthesia.

The clinic hero's circle of friends continues to grow. Maui adores a rabbit named Gracie who is also boarded at the vet's office and often cries to be let into her cage. And she has no problems with felines, according to Orlowski-Smith, "Kittens are the bomb for her." But Maui's favorite companion is Maple, whom Orlowski-Smith and her husband adopted six months after Maui. "As long as Maple is there, everything's good for Maui," says Orlowski-Smith of the happy duo.

Maple's gift to the office is her sensitivity toward stressed owners. "If there is someone sitting in the lobby who is finding out some bad news or putting down a dog, you'll find Maple's head in their lap," says Orlowski-Smith. "Maple senses when you're sad and she's right on you."

At home, the two dogs pass their days playing on the 160 acres of farm land that surround them, or lying on the couch with the family cat. In the summer, Maui enjoys riding a float in the pool, while Maple watches from the steps. Of her unlikely all-stars, Orlowski-Smith says, "I don't think you necessarily find the dog you want. But you find the dog you need." ◆

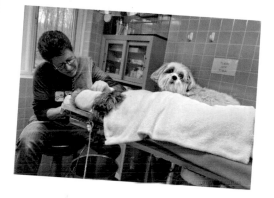

MAUI KEEPS WATCH (LEFT) AS HER OWNER, VETERINARY ASSISTANT LINDA ORLOWSKI-SMITH, OPERATES ON A PATIENT. THE LITTLE DOG'S ATTENTIVE PRESENCE CALMS THE ANXIOUS ANIMALS AND PET OWNERS THAT PASS THROUGH THE VETERINARY CLINIC.

LOVE IS BLIND: *After losing his sight to an infection, Smiley was a particularly destructive puppy. But thanks to an owner who believed in second chances, he grew into a star therapy dog.*

# SMILEY

## SEEING WITH HIS HEART

### Golden retriever •—• Ontario, Canada

Joanne George was working as a veterinary technician and dog trainer outside of Toronto more than a decade ago, when her office received a call from a backyard breeder. The breeder had more than a hundred golden retrievers of varying ages, many of which were in terrible health, and the authorities had ordered her to seek immediate medical care for all of the dogs.

Instead, the breeder decided to euthanize 20 dogs and called George's office to request their services. The vet staff, in turn, was determined to rescue the animals and divvy them up into homes.

As the most seasoned caretaker with many years of experience fostering rescue dogs, George was assigned the blind two-year-old golden retriever whose eyes were oozing with infection. George dubbed her new pet Smiley, although the dog didn't give her family much to smile about when she first brought him home. Despite being the first animal to get along with Tyler, their rambunctious albino Great Dane, Smiley was destructive. The constant pain from his infection compelled the golden retriever to act out. He destroyed an entire leather couch before turning his attention to each and every electrical cord he could find.

Smiley wasn't house-trained or crate-trained. If he was left in a crate, he would panic, make a mess, and emerge covered in his own waste. It was easier to clean the house than to bathe Smiley on a daily basis, so the unruly guest was left to his own devices while George was at work. But after six months, George grew weary of the chaos. She decided to make Smiley her constant companion so that she could guide him toward better behavior. "You're going to be a very busy dog," George remembers telling the unwitting canine.

George didn't bother wasting time on basic commands like "sit," since Smiley required a tailored approach. She patiently taught her blind puppy commands that are necessary for him, like how to hop into her SUV by George tapping on the back of the car three times so Smiley might put his paws up and gauge how far he had to leap. Smiley quickly learned to dismount with grace as well. George next educated him about the perimeters of the porch so he wouldn't fall off. She led him up and down the staircase until he could navigate it by himself. He went to work with her; he went to visit her grandmother in a nursing home; he visited with the other nursing home residents and, frankly, anyone else who crossed their paths. Gradually, Smiley became an ideal companion, and George realized that Smiley was going to stay, and he was going to do good.

**GRADUALLY, SMILEY BECAME AN IDEAL COMPANION . . . SMILEY WAS GOING TO STAY, AND HE WAS GOING TO DO GOOD.**

Smiley, who had surgery to suture his eyelids shut so they ceased being infected, immediately took to paying it forward. George remembers that when she brought Smiley for his therapy dog test, the evaluator approached her at the end with tears

OWNER JOANNE GEORGE (LEFT) DEVISED CREATIVE WAYS TO TRAIN SMILEY WITH AUDITORY CUES AND BY LETTING HIM ACCOMPANY HER EVERYWHERE SHE WENT. CHILDREN ARE PARTICULARLY DRAWN TO THE DOG'S GENTLE NATURE AND LOVING PERSONALITY.

"I TALK ABOUT HOW IT ISN'T SMILEY'S FAULT THAT HE WAS BORN DIFFERENT. WE ARE ALL DIFFERENT, IN SOME WAY, EVEN IF IT'S [SOMETHING AS SIMPLE AS] HAVING RED HAIR."

in her eyes. George expected the worse. Now an evaluator of therapy dogs herself, George understands that reaction. "She knew he was going to be a very, very special dog who would change people's lives. He's got something magical about him."

For more than a decade, George and Smiley have inspired people with their story, which has spread through a huge social media following. Despite their international outreach—fans as far as India write about how Smiley has given them the courage to be themselves—the pair's favorite volunteer work is local. George sees the golden retriever making a profound impact at an elementary school, where Smiley reminds children that everyone has to work harder at certain tasks. The beloved dog is a living lesson in many ways, explains his handler: "I talk about how it isn't Smiley's fault that he was born different. We are all different, in some way, even if it's [something as simple as] having red hair." The students take the anti-bullying message to heart when it comes from Smiley.

Smiley is a senior dog now, but George keeps him volunteering, believing that everyone—humans and animals alike—need a job to fulfill them until the end. And indeed, no matter what he does, this unlikely icon will continue to show that everyone has something to give back, even if it's as simple as a smile. ◆

SNUGGLE BUDDIES: *Naptime is a sacred time. When bashful Nora was adopted, she quickly bonded with her family's infant son, Archie, proving that friendship knows no bounds.*

# NORA

## STRIKING A POSE

### English pointer ⊷ Manitoba, Canada

Nora did not possess the obvious qualities of a social media star. Rescued from a puppy mill where she had been kept outdoors for all 10 months of her life, the English pointer was undernourished and frightened when Elizabeth Spence and her husband, Mike Aporius, met her at Funds for Furry Friends shelter in Manitoba, Canada.

"She was the most pitiful thing I have ever seen," remembers Elizabeth. Although not even a year old, Nora had recently given birth, and her puppies were available for adoption. The newborns were a far easier sell, but Nora won the couple's hearts. "She came and laid in my arms and that was that," Elizabeth describes. "You could tell she was the sweetest thing."

Nora joined the household, which at the time included several other family pets. Gradually, the timid pointer settled in, learning to walk up and down stairs and finding her place in the pack. She also found a place in the master bedroom. Spence remembers, "When we got her, we said we'd never have dogs in the bed. But that first night she jumped up, and I got her down." After this fruitless exercise was repeated five times, Nora stayed on the bed. She has been there ever since.

Nora's family continued to expand after her arrival: They now have three children in addition to three rescue cats and two dogs. Nora's attachment to the youngest child, Archie, is so remarkable that Spence began to take pictures of the pair napping and snuggling together. She posted the photographs on Instagram (@wellettas), and thousands of strangers gravitated toward the images, drawn in by the charming resemblance between Nora and Archie and the innocence of their friendship.

"She's equally devoted to all the kids, but I think she's especially drawn to Archie because he's an extremely laid back, quiet baby," says Spence, who reports that thunderstorms and loud noises still cause the skittish dog to hide under the bed or behind the toilet. The popularity of her portraits continues to surprise Spence, since for her the scenes are just everyday reality in her home: "Animals and kids are always in a pile everywhere."

## "NORA'S SURROUNDED BY LOVE NOW."

One more creature has joined the pileup, thanks to the Spence's open-door (and open-heart) policy: They adopted Remington, one of Nora's daughters, when her first adoptive family moved to Europe and was unable to bring her. Nora and Remington seemed to recognize each other immediately: When they met again, they did a little dance together before Remington put her paw on Nora's head and Nora lay down. "It's the most beautiful relationship," Spence says of the pair, who can be seen contentedly lounging or playing together in many of her photographs. ◆

ARCHIE AND NORA REMAINED INSEPARABLE AS HE GREW FROM A BABY (LEFT) TO A TODDLER (BELOW). THE FAMILY ALSO ADOPTED ONE OF NORA'S PUPPIES, REMINGTON, WHOM SHE SEEMED TO RECOGNIZE DESPITE A LONG SEPARATION.

**FRIENDSHIP FORGED IN FIRE:** *Jake has scars from when he was trapped in a burning shed, but he gained a steadfast friend in William Lindler, the firefighter who rescued him from the flames.*

# HONORARY FIREFIGHTER

### Pit bull ➺ South Carolina

Firefighter William Lindler was off duty when he saw his neighbor's shed go up in flames. "There are dogs in there!" yelled the neighbor. Lindler grabbed his gear from his pickup truck and was soon joined by the members of his fire station in Hanahan, South Carolina.

As they worked to put the fire out, a pit bull and some of her three-week-old puppies fled the building, but one puppy, Jake, became trapped under a piece of burning wood that fell from the ceiling. When he finally freed himself, the disoriented dog ran deeper into the smoke and flames.

It took the firefighters at least 10 minutes to control the fire enough to reach the pup. The tiny dog wasn't breathing. "These were conditions most people would have perished in," says Lindler, a former Marine with experience as a K9 handler. Lindler performed mouth-to-snout CPR on Jake until he began to breathe; he then gave him a pet oxygen mask and wrapped him in a wet towel. A firefighter from a neighboring station offered to drive Jake to an emergency veterinarian clinic nearby.

Second- and third-degree burns covered more than 70 percent of Jake's body, a condition so severe that the Animal Medical Clinic of Goose Creek did not have a treatment protocol. But the crew administered a morphine drip for the pain and agreed to try their best.

When Lindler went to visit Jake a couple of days later, the vet told him that the owners were unable to take responsibility for his care, and the vet was reclassifying him as an abandoned pet. Without thinking, Lindler heard himself reply, "He's not abandoned. My wife and I will take care of the bills and of him."

The clinic met Lindler's act of kindness with its own: Every dollar of Jake's treatment—which involved two months of a morphine drip, around-the-clock medication, twice-daily baths, and laser therapy to care for his skin—was covered by an "angel fund" through the vet's office. Determined to pay it all back, Lindler fundraises on Jake's Facebook page, where he also brings attention to local shelter dogs in need of adoption.

After three months of intensive rehabilitation, Jake was ready to go home. But the puppy still needed constant care, so Lindler asked his chief if he could bring the dog to work. Soon enough, the recovering pit bull was not only keeping the firefighters company at the station, but in true fire-dog fashion, he also joined them on the truck when they got a call. Jake also charmed the employees at the town hall, many of whom started carrying treats and paying regular visits to see the community pet. Soon enough, the city was swearing in the popular puppy as an honorary firefighter in an official town hall ceremony.

Now fully recovered, Jake spends more time at home with his canine sister, Bella, the Lindler family's Rottweiler. Lindler planned for Jake to train as a therapy dog for burn victims, but he now believes that the pit bull's energy and drive to work might make him a better arson detective dog. While Lindler saves to pay for the training, he continues to take Jake to events, and they visit schools for fire prevention week. "He is," says Lindler, "loving life." ◆

THOUGH BURNS COVERED 70 PERCENT OF HIS BODY AS A PUPPY (ABOVE), JAKE IS NOW HAPPY AND HEALTHY. HE SPENT SO MUCH TIME AT THE FIRE STATION DURING HIS TREATMENT THAT HE WAS EVENTUALLY SWORN IN AS AN HONORARY FIREFIGHTER.

PAWS WITH A CAUSE: *Little Fred gave his owner the courage to stand up to a severe illness, and they now act as a team, campaigning for health care for HIV-positive teens.*

# FRED

## HEALING A DOCTOR

### Yorkshire terrier ⋈ Illinois

**W**ithin 18 months, Robert Garofalo was assaulted, split from his partner of more than a decade, underwent treatment for cancer, and was diagnosed with HIV. The physician at Chicago's Lurie Children's Hospital, who specializes in adolescent medicine and treats marginalized populations—including HIV-positive and LGBT patients—spiraled into a depression.

"I fell into a dark place," he says. He was coming home to an empty apartment for the first time in years, experiencing post-traumatic stress from being attacked, and was disconsolate at learning he was HIV-positive. "What comes with an HIV diagnosis for many is a lot of shame and guilt and self-imposed isolation, and I really lost myself to that dynamic," Garofalo recalls. Even with every resource available to him, he describes a feeling of not knowing where to turn. "I never could afford myself the same compassion I've taught others."

On a trip to visit his mother in New Jersey, the Chicago resident stayed mum about his diagnosis, as he had with everyone else in his life. But as they said their goodbyes at the airport, Garofalo's mother put her hands on his face and told him that she felt something was wrong. She promised him that while he couldn't talk about it then, she knew that one day he would be able to share what was troubling him, and he would then feel better.

Garofalo sobbed the entire way home. That night, sitting at his computer, he faced a crushing depression that made him doubt his immediate survival. In a moment of clarity that he still can't explain, a thought occurred: Maybe I should get a dog. Garofalo had never had a dog before, and when he called his best friend to test the idea, his reaction was hesitant: "You can't even take care of yourself. How are you going to take care of a dog?" he asked. But Garofalo knew he had to try something, so he typed "puppies in Chicago" into a Google search, and up popped a picture of Fred.

Two days later, the Yorkshire terrier puppy was in his new home, and immediately, Garofalo felt a sense of purpose, even though he admits he had no idea what to do with his new companion. Still, he says he never experienced a moment of feeling overwhelmed by the responsibility. "I had this little creature who needed me, but I needed him more," Garofalo remembers. "There was a purity to his soul that was palpable, and I had to be accountable to him. From the beginning, I wanted to do better for him."

Garofalo had been suffering night terrors as a result of PTSD from his assault, and he would often wake up screaming. He would find a startled Fred cowering under the bed, and sometimes it took hours to coax him out. Slowly, and surely, the night terrors stopped. And eventually, the depression and anxiety abated. Much to Garofalo's amazement, he began to feel both peace and joy again, simply through the act of coming home to a loving companion. "We developed this relationship out of need and despair and love, and soon we became inseparable," Garofalo remembers. "And within a month or two I began to feel I wasn't alone anymore. The apartment had felt like a tomb without my partner, but with Fred, there was another source of energy."

EVEN ON THE LONELIEST DAYS, ROB GAROFALO (LEFT) FOUND A SOURCE OF COMFORT AND JOY IN FRED. BELOW, FRED SITS WITH A TOY MADE IN HIS IMAGE THAT THEY WILL SELL TO SUPPORT HIS NAMESAKE ORGANIZATION, FRED SAYS.

It's an energy that is perfect for the doctor, who admits he's high-strung, a characteristic that's also usually associated with Yorkies. But Fred knows how to calm his owner, too. "When I come home from work, sometimes he'll look at me as if to say, 'Bring it down a notch.' Fred is a natural stress diffuser for me." And even though Fred only cuddles on his own terms, his presence is no less sweet: "I love when he snores," Garofalo says. "It is the cutest and most comforting sound to me. It means he is at peace and that means I have done my job."

**"BECAUSE I DON'T THINK I WOULD HAVE *HAD* A JOURNEY WITHOUT HIM." LET ALONE ONE FILLED WITH SUCH JOY.**

Several months after Fred arrived, Garofalo returned to visit his mother. This time he brought Fred—and the courage to let his mother know about his diagnosis. One morning, he overheard his mother telling Fred that he was a miracle because he had brought her son back. In that moment, Garofalo determined that he and his dog would be of service to others. "[Fred] got my silly back, he got my mojo back, he got my spirit back," he says, and he believed that the special Yorkie could be the face of similar inspiration to other people in need.

The physician did some research on social media and discovered a dog who had accumulated 19 million Facebook friends by simply looking charming dressed in hats and sunglasses. The dog had also raised a million dollars for charity. "I thought, 'My dog's cuter than that,'" Garofalo says jokingly.

At first, some of his friends and colleagues laughed off the idea that Fred could support HIV charities, and Garofalo's initial idea—selling greeting cards with the dog's picture on them—was a bust. Still determined to make an impact, Garofalo started the nonprofit Fred Says, and eventually the pair hit their stride thanks to community support. By fund-raising through bike rides, Fred Says donated more than $200,000 in its first four years to care and services for HIV-positive youth.

Garofalo's experience also inspired him to team up with a writer and photographer to cross the country interviewing and visually documenting people who are HIV-positive, along with their four-legged companions. The result is the traveling exhibition "When Dogs Heal." Each portrait is accompanied by a first-person narrative about the subject's journey with the disease and how the dogs have impacted their owner's lives. Garofalo chose not to include his own story in the exhibition to keep the spotlight on other participants, but he recognizes that Fred is at the center of it all. "I can't talk about my journey without it being about him," Garofalo says. "Because I don't think I would have *had* a journey without him." Let alone one filled with such joy. ◆

**LOVE UNCHAINED:** *Hope was rescued by an EMS unit who couldn't bear to give her up—so they didn't! She moved into the station, cheering the busy paramedics with a wagging tail and wide smile.*

# HOPE

## KNOWING HER STATION

### Australian cattle dog ⊷ Pennsylvania

Courtney Ivan had long been a dog lover, so one day when the EMS paramedic responded to a call at the home of someone who had died, she wasn't put off by the police who told her to keep a distance from the "aggressive" Australian cattle dog chained up nearby. Instead, Ivan sat on the porch and played with the dog while she waited for the police to finish up inside.

Ivan, who has seven dogs of her own at home in Hermitage, Pennsylvania, was already calling shelters to see if anyone could take the dog in when she noticed the dog's limp. Recognizing that the cattle dog would need medical attention, Ivan contacted the local humane society instead. They agreed to take the dog the next day, but until then the dog would stay at the station with Ivan as she finished her 24-hour shift. The injured canine would have the good company of Humphrey, a rescue dog who lived at the station full-time.

When it came time for Ivan to deliver the cattle dog to the humane society, she found that her colleagues had other plans. She discovered two matching dog beds, two matching collars, and a group of EMS staff informing her that they'd named the dog Hope and she was there to stay.

It wasn't an easy transition for all of them. Hope immediately bonded with Humphrey, but she was distrustful of the men in the station. They helped ease the situation by lying on the floor with Hope, allowing her to approach them until she was so comfortable she was lying on top of them.

But months later, Hope began showing signs of aggression. A few visits to the vet made it clear that Hope was in terrible pain. With multiple fractures, likely caused by sustained abuse, Hope's leg was useless. The vet recommended an amputation. "I cried all night having to make that call," Ivan remembers. "But I knew it was the right one. The vet said it was like she was carrying a ball and chain behind her."

After surgery, Hope returned to find the station converted into a recovery home for her. The bunk room, where the paramedics can rest during their 24-hour shifts, had been upturned; the bunk beds were taken apart and a single mattress laid on the floor for the mending pet. Long since healed, Hope's room remains the same. It is now Hope and Humphrey's bedroom, which they graciously share with the humans who wander in.

The reward for the station is a dog who, along with Humphrey, helps ease the burden of their days. "We all realized when Hope was at the hospital that something was missing," says Ivan. "When you come back, and they hear the car turn into the lot, you hear them barking and you are met by them with their little butts wiggling." When a team returns from a particularly difficult call, no matter how many other colleagues are in the room, the dogs sense their emotions and go straight to their side. After a long day serving others, it's nice to accept help from a friend—especially large furry friends who lay their heads in your lap.

The only downside to Hope's affection, says Ivan, is the challenge of getting work done at the station. When Hope wants attention, she crawls on top of Ivan's computer and lies down on top of it—a most endearing excuse for procrastination. ◆

ONE OF HOPE'S LEGS WAS IRREP-
ARABLY FRACTURED FROM ABUSIVE
CONDITIONS IN HER EARLY LIFE,
SO OWNER COURTNEY IVAN (LEFT)
HAD TO MAKE THE TOUGH DECISION
TO AMPUTATE. LUCKILY, HOPE'S
BOUNDLESS AFFECTION REMAINS
UNDIMINISHED.

UNDEFEATED: *Caroline Dimmer had only signed up to volunteer at a pit bull rescue, but she found her perfect match in Olivia, a former fighting-ring dog with inspiring resilience.*

# OLIVIA

## A REAL WINNER

### Pit bull •—• Florida

Olivia has been the ultimate face of peace since Plenty of Pit Bulls rescued the former fighting-ring dog in Gainesville, Florida. The affectionate pup enchanted volunteers as she was nursed back to health, and her joy proved particularly irresistible to one woman.

Caroline Dimmer had fostered rescue dogs until her graduate school work made it prohibitive. When Dimmer heard that Plenty of Pit Bulls was looking for volunteers, she asked if she might be of service. Meanwhile, Olivia's foster had fallen through and she was in boarding, a terrible situation for any dog, but especially for one with a traumatic past whose adoption could depend on ongoing socialization.

When Dimmer showed up at the boarding facility to spend time with Olivia, the visit turned into an eight-hour play date instead. "I never wanted to take her back," Dimmer remembers. "She was the sweetest, most loving dog." Two days later, Dimmer took Olivia home and the ever smiling pit bull never left.

Olivia, who loves dogs, cats, horses, and humans, soon became a registered therapy dog, appearing at educational events and volunteering at a hospital. Her favorite post is at a library where children read to her while she lies contentedly on her back, one of the only positions in which she isn't constantly wagging her tail. ◆

SENIOR MOMENT: *White-whiskered Pops maintains a lively personality in his old age. He helps his owner, a retired Vietnam veteran, engage with their neighbors and Detroit community.*

# POPS

## THE UNLIKELY COUPLE

### Chihuahua ➼ Michigan

Pops rounded the corner in the nick of time. Joel Rockey, founder of One Last Treat, an organization that pairs senior dogs with veterans, was just getting ready to leave the Animal Control center in Ridgecrest, California, when he encountered the Chihuahua in the hallway. The U.S. Navy combat medic had filled his rescue quota, but there was something about Pops—Rockey describes it as an almost human look in his eyes—and he knew he couldn't leave the old dog behind.

Rockey was at the tail end of a cross-country road trip from Michigan to California, in which he had rescued 22 shelter dogs in as many days—a number meant to reflect the number of veterans who commit suicide every day.

Back in Michigan, Rockey received a request for a dog from a Vietnam veteran in Detroit named Greg Brabaw. Brabaw explained that he lived alone and was looking for a companion to relieve his boredom. But when Rockey offered that he had a Chihuahua who might be a perfect match, Brabaw paused. "I was prejudiced then," he remembers. "I wasn't high on Chihuahuas."

Unfazed, Rockey pressed his case. He saw that Brabaw was witty and fun loving, just the character to match Pops's personality. "I figured these two could get into trouble together," Rockey recalls. He also explained to Brabaw that senior dogs are difficult to adopt, and that if he were willing, he could give Pops "one last little hurrah." Finally, Brabaw agreed.

Pops was aloof when he first arrived at Brabaw's apartment. But after a couple of weeks, he seemed to understand he was finally at home and warmed up to his new owner. For Brabaw, the dog's presence was immediately powerful. He had been spending the majority of his time alone, and now he was taking the dog for walks and speaking with people on the street about him. His neighbor, a woman he had never met before, approached him to tell him that she had seen the pair on the Facebook page of One Last Treat. "People in my age and position are introverted and stay in their apartments, so that was cool," he says.

In fact, rescuing Pops has widened Brabaw's community well beyond the block where he lives. Rockey and his colleagues have become good friends with their fellow veteran, often dropping in on Brabaw and taking him out for meals.

For his part, Pops has proven to be an affectionate companion, covering his owner in kisses and greeting him with a joyful race around the dining room table each time he returns home. Brabaw has reveled in teaching tricks to Pops—whom he describes as "smart as a whip"—and in rewarding him with treats. Perhaps too many treats. Asked if the dog is in good shape, Brabaw answers, "He's in very good shape. If round is a shape."

The relationship is a win for everyone involved, according to Rockey. There are so many animals in need, and in his experience, retirement-age veterans welcome the task of caring for a pet and again answer the call to contribute to a greater good. Brabaw certainly does. "It's Pops's last hurrah, and I'm pretty sure it's mine, too," he jokes. "Since I got him, I feel better about everything." Apparently, so does the rotund Chihuahua, whose final act has proven to include not one, but *many* last treats. ◆

BRABAW HAS REVELED IN TEACHING
TRICKS TO POPS—WHOM HE DESCRIBES
AS "SMART AS A WHIP"—AND IN
REWARDING HIM WITH TREATS.
PERHAPS TOO MANY TREATS.
ASKED IF THE DOG IS IN GOOD SHAPE,
BRABAW ANSWERS, "HE'S IN VERY
GOOD SHAPE. IF ROUND IS A SHAPE."

HEARTHROB: *The Instagram account @Tunameltsmyheart captures Tuna's ability to be a total goofball yet irresistibly sincere at the same time. This snapshot was posted for Valentine's Day.*

# TUNA

## A WINNING SMILE

### Chiweenie ⋈ California

Tuna still had his baby teeth when Courtney Dasher saw him at a farmer's market, where a rescuer was soliciting his adoption. The shy Chiweenie was shivering in the outdoor chill, so the rescuers had wrapped him in an oversized sweatshirt. Dasher—who had no experience fostering rescue dogs—decided at the moment for reasons she still doesn't understand that she would volunteer.

Dasher spent about a week trying to get the dog adopted, but even with his few Chiclet teeth, the Chihuahua-dachshund mix was still a hard, funny-looking sell. During that time, Dasher felt her resolve start to soften, particularly when she woke up one morning to find that the pup had slept on her shoulder. Still, she told the rescuer that she couldn't adopt him because of her busy schedule. The rescuer responded with an analogy about people who get pregnant unintentionally and find their lives positively transformed: Dasher recalls her saying, "Like those situations, adopting him will change your life." Those words would prove prophetic.

As Tuna made himself at home with Dasher, his adult teeth slowly came in, a situation that she describes as "very interesting dentistry." With a profound over-bite, Tuna has to chew with his back molars and has a difficult time drinking water if the bowl is too deep. The dog's unique smile is likely a result of inbreeding or crossbreeding but it is a harmless condition that has only made him more photogenic: After a year of posting photos of Tuna to her Instagram feed, the handle went viral. With nearly two million followers, @Tunameltsmyheart has allowed Dasher to quit her job to manage her celebrity pet full-time. She directs all Tuna's attention back to animal welfare, helping raise awareness and financial support for dog rescue organizations.

Tuna's happy to champion the cause, as long as the efforts don't involve children. The Chiweenie much prefers the company of adults to kids and becomes uncomfortable when young ones are around. "Luckily our demographic is women between 25 and 34," Dasher says with a laugh. "Every once in a while a child is there, and we deal with it, but there's never a time when he's not snarky."

Tuna's ideal day, however, would be spent under the covers, an attribute Dasher says makes him the ideal boss. "He sleeps all day and lets me do whatever I want." ◆

TUNA IS A DACHSHUND-
CHIHUAHUA CROSSBREED
WITH AN OVERBITE THAT
IS COMPLETELY NATURAL—
AND NATURALLY ADORABLE.
HE ENJOYS NAPPING WITH
HIS FAVORITE MONSTER
TOY (LEFT) AND BEING HIS
HANDSOME SELF.

GOING THE DISTANCE: *The Andrawos family was forced to leave their beloved dog behind when they fled Aleppo. After a miraculous reunion, Fox has become a symbol of hope for their new life.*

# FOX

## FROM WAR TO PEACE

### Swiss shepherd–poodle mix ⊷ Quebec, Canada

"**D**ear Mrs. Lori,"begins the email to SPCA International's program manager: *"I am Gaby Andrawos. I left Syria urgently with my mom Nicole Haffar and my brother Namir, but we left our lovely dog Fox . . ."*

Hooked, Lori Kalef read on: *"We left him with my dad in a very dangerous area. Please help us bring our Fox. My mom is always crying. She is extremely worried about Fox. I can't find the words to thank you in advance."*

The letter came from Montreal, where Andrawos and his family had finally relocated. Seventeen months earlier, Gaby, his brother, and his mother had fled the civil war in Aleppo, Syria. They were forced to make the gut-wrenching decision to leave behind their careers and their family, including their father, immobilized by polio, and their grandmother who suffers from dementia. And, of course, there was the beloved Fox, their Swiss shepherd–poodle mix, to consider.

On September 25, 2014, a missile hit the Andrawos home, blowing off the roof. Months later, Gaby, his brother, and his mother received their immigration papers and prepared to make the journey to Beirut. There, they would wait for permission to enter Canada, with the sponsorship of Gaby's aunt. It was impossible to take their father, who stayed behind to care for their grandmother, or their dog on a trip that required them to elude both Al Qaeda and ISIS, so the family was forced to split up.

The sons and their mother spent a year in Beirut, where they were able to work and—what's most important, says Gaby—live in a familiar culture and language. That would all change in December 2015, when they arrived in Montreal. Speaking only Arabic at the time, Gaby says the adaptation was difficult: "We didn't have language to communicate or to be independent, and we prize our independence." His mother, now unemployed, became increasingly homesick. Gaby promised her that he would find a way to get their dog. "After four years of war in Syria, I needed to see my mother have mental and physical good health," he says. "And Fox was the happiness in her heart."

When Gaby's request came through to Kalef at the SPCA, she agreed on the spot—even if she was not exactly sure how the organization was going to make it happen. She and her colleagues were committed to trying, as previously the team had pulled hundreds of animals out of war-torn countries, typically upon the request of U.S. service members. "We've never said no to an animal," Kalef declares. "And certainly not to an animal and human reuniting." For the Andrawos family, "It was the beginning of the happiness for us, of a dream coming true," as Gaby puts it.

Kalef called an urgent meeting and gave research assignments to the team members. They discovered an organization called Syrian Animal Rescue Association (SARA), based in Damascus, and contacted them to say that they would fund the mission to rescue Fox at all costs, as long as no one was put in danger.

Weeks later, a volunteer was scheduled to drive from Damascus to Aleppo in the middle of the night to get the dog, but the mission had to be aborted due to imminent danger in the area. The next day, another volunteer stepped forward to make the journey, and Fox was spirited out of Aleppo. "We weren't able to sleep, we were

"AFTER FOUR YEARS OF WAR
IN SYRIA, I NEEDED TO SEE
MY MOTHER HAVE MENTAL
AND PHYSICAL GOOD HEALTH . . .
AND FOX WAS THE HAPPINESS
IN HER HEART."

so anxious," says Gaby. "Now it seems funny how nervous we were, but it was really, really awful then."

Fox spent several days in Damascus before Beirut for the Ethical Treatment of Animals (BETA) stepped in to help and agreed to meet the dog at the border. Also joining them was the owner of Woof Airlines, an international pet transport company, who was so moved by Fox's story that he had agreed to personally fly the dog from Beirut to Montreal.

**"BUT IN THAT MOMENT, SEEING FOX WAS LIKE A LIGHT—A LIGHT THAT MADE IT ALL DISAPPEAR FOR ONE SECOND."**

Four months after first contacting the SPCA, Gaby—along with his mother, brother, and aunt—headed to the airport to pick up their dog. "We have all the misery that we saw in Syria, and all the worry for our father and grandmother and everyone still in Aleppo," says Gaby. "But in that moment, seeing Fox was like a light—a light that made it all disappear for one second."

For his part, Fox has had no discernible issues adjusting to his new home. He is back to sleeping in Mrs. Andrawos's bed and has made many new dog friends in Montreal. He's completely Canadian now, according to his family. Better yet, he has the freedom to do whatever he likes, whenever he likes, or as Gaby says, "He knows his rights."

The touching airport reunion will not soon be forgotten. To Kalef, who was meeting the Andrawos family in person for the first time, it was the start of an enduring friendship. And for the family, it was a sign of hope. "Something very important was missing for us," says Gaby. "Now, we can start to live our lives slowly, step by step. Now, we can have something like peace." ◆

A STAFF MEMBER OF SPCA INTERNATIONAL (LEFT) COMPLETES THE FINAL HAND-OFF AT THE MONTREAL AIRPORT, WHERE FOX'S FAMILY WAS JOYFULLY REUNITED WITH THEIR PET. THEY LIVED THROUGH FOUR YEARS OF WAR IN SYRIA BEFORE FINDING SAFETY IN CANADA.

LATE BLOOMER: *Olive was painfully shy when she was adopted, and she lost all her teeth after an infection, but she blossomed into the spirited mascot of her owner's dog-care radio show.*

# OLIVE

## A DOGGY DIVA

### Italian greyhound ⊷ Florida

Olive seemed the least likely candidate to be the spokesdog for a radio show called *The Doggy Diva Show*. The weekly pet-care broadcast was launched by Floridian Susan Marie Campbell to advocate for rescued animals like her own greyhound, Sophia, the original face of the show.

After Sophia passed away, Campbell continued the radio show without a muse. Then, she was involved in a tractor-trailer accident that resulted in a myriad of operations and hospitalizations. She found herself increasingly isolated and too frightened to drive herself anywhere.

When a rescue organization called and asked if she would be willing to adopt a three-legged Italian greyhound, she agreed to meet Olive. The rescue was looking for someone with experience handling a three-legged dog, and Campbell already owned a greyhound who had lost a leg years ago. The ideal adopter would also be home most of the time to meet the dog's needs for socialization.

It took months for Olive—the victim of neglect by a backyard breeder—to even wag her tail. All of her teeth had to be removed because of an infection, and her leg had been amputated shortly after her rescue due to cancer. She was completely traumatized, says Campbell. "But I thought I could help her. I never realized Olive would help me."

As she focused on nursing Olive back to health, Campbell not only began leaving the house again, but she also insisted on driving herself. "I got back out. She was my healer." In addition to her motivating effect, Olive has turned out to be an untrained medical alert dog for Campbell's crippling migraines. Campbell discovered that the usually quiet dog cries half an hour before the onset of a migraine, which gives her the time she needs to head it off.

## "SHE'S BROUGHT ME A SENSE OF CONFIDENCE . . . AND SHE'S BROUGHT JOY BACK INTO MY LIFE."

"She's brought me a sense of confidence," says Campbell. "And she's brought joy back into my life." Not to mention spreading that happiness to others as the new face of the *The Doggy Diva Show*, enlivening the segment's Facebook page with photos of her dressed in various costumes. With a tongue that is always hanging out because of her lack of teeth, Olive has a most distinctive look. As Campbell says, it is the look of unconditional love. ◆

SUSAN MARIE CAMPBELL WAS RECOVERING FROM SURGERY WHEN SHE FIRST ADOPTED OLIVE. THE DOG BECAME HER CONSTANT COMPANION, ACTING AS AN UNTRAINED MEDICAL ALERT DOG AND EVEN JOINING HER IN THE RECORDING STUDIO (BELOW).

LIGHT IN THE DARK: *Bruschi lost both of his eyes to two separate medical complications, leaving him completely blind by age three—but that hasn't kept this pup from smiling and spreading love.*

# BRUSCHI

## A CHAMPION COMEBACK

### Pit bull mix •—• Arizona

**B**ruschi, a nearly blind pit bull whose littermates had already been adopted, was in need of a home with specific requirements: a family with experience caring for a visually impaired dog, an older dog to help show him the ropes, and preferably no children, whose loud noises might scare him. But there was no telling how long Bruschi might be waiting for his Goldilocks family at the Arizona Animal Welfare League.

Meanwhile, in nearby Phoenix, Meridith and Jack Doucette were watching the local CBS station's segment on adopting a pet. They only needed one look to fall in love with Bruschi, who was being profiled on the segment. Their instant attraction was catapulted into action when Meridith went online and read the description of the puppy's desired home. The Doucettes had raised a terrier mix who was blind from complications with diabetes, and their family included an older Labrador and no young children. It was a perfect match, so Meridith called the shelter.

At the time, Bruschi happened to be in the infirmary for kennel cough, but that didn't deter the patient Doucettes. Meridith called the shelter daily until they were allowed to bring Bruschi home. To keep the small puppy warm, the couple wrapped him in a blanket. Even as a grown adult, Bruschi still likes to be tucked in at night and will wander the house with a blanket draped over him.

The Doucettes gave their spirited pet the name Bruschi after former Patriots player Tedy Bruschi, who suffered a stroke but persevered to be back on the field within a year. Their feisty and clever puppy deserved a strong name, and, like the athlete, Bruschi seemed undaunted by what could have been a crippling disability. He graduated first in his obedience class after the teacher modified commands to be auditory rather than visual.

## BRUSCHI SEEMED UNDAUNTED BY WHAT COULD HAVE BEEN A CRIPPLING DISABILITY.

At age three, Bruschi caught Valley Fever, a fungal disease that resulted in the removal of one of his eyes. A month later, glaucoma necessitated the removal of his other eye. Meridith took time off from work to nurse the dog back to health. Most animals loathe the plastic cones they wear after surgery, but for Bruschi it was even more restricting, according to Meridith: "Because Bruschi's blind, he thinks he's paralyzed and can't move. Or maybe that's just him."

Nevertheless, the determined canine was soon back to romping in the dog run, where a simple correction of "Careful!" alerts him that he is headed for the fence or another obstacle. At home, he plays tug-of-war with the Doucettes' more recent adoptee, a terrier mix named Caroline. The new friend brings a rope toy over to Bruschi and bumps it into his chest to get his attention and to let him know it's time to play.

Bruschi frequently attends adoption and pet events where his goofy smile and demeanor change people's minds, not only about the pit bull breed but also about dogs with disabilities. At one event, a boy with autism asked to pet Bruschi,

AS A PUPPY, BRUSCHI NEEDED TO BE SWADDLED TO BE KEPT WARM (LEFT). NOW WARMTH RADIATES FROM HIM TOWARD FAMILIES HE MEETS WHILE HELPING TO CHANGE THE PUBLIC PERCEPTION OF PIT BULLS AND DOGS WITH DISABILITIES (ABOVE).

"[BRUSCHI] AND HIS FAMILY EXEMPLIFY EVERYTHING ABOUT THE BOND BETWEEN ANIMALS AND HUMANS. HERE IS A DOG WHO HAS GONE THROUGH EVERYTHING, AND HE'S MORE THAN JUST HAPPY–HE IS *LIGHT*."

commenting that he had no eyes. Meridith recalls, "The mother responded, 'He's special, like you,' and the boy's eyes lit up." The boy repeated the words "special like me," and in an instant a bond was formed. Bruschi is a source of inspiration for many people who meet him, Meridith says.

And in fact, Bruschi's story won the "Write your rescue story" contest that the Arizona Animal Welfare League & SPCA initiated, and it became a cornerstone of their fund-raising efforts. "There were so many amazing stories about great people and great dogs," says League spokesperson Michael Morefield. "But [Bruschi] and his family exemplify everything about the bond between animals and humans. Here is a dog who has gone through everything, and he's more than just happy—he is *light*." ◆

TINY DANCER: *Nathan was a particularly challenging foster dog. Eventually, though, he not only found his forever home but a hidden talent as well—he's a great dancer!*

# NATHAN

## KEEPING THE BEAT

### Hairless Chinese crested ✦ Virginia

**N**athan could steal the spotlight on *Dancing With the Stars*, but this sure-footed dog wasn't always so easy to love. At six years old, he landed in a shelter after his elderly owner could no longer care for him.

Nathan was distrustful of strangers, particularly men, and he had no reservations about expressing it with a swift bite to the ankle. So began a pattern of short-lived rehoming until a South Carolina organization called Bald Is Beautiful—a rescue for hairless and small dogs—intervened. They reached out to Tina Hicks in Seaford, Virginia. Hicks already had five other dogs, but with years of fostering experience and no man in the house, the hope was that Hicks could socialize Nathan and give him a chance at a sustainable adoption.

Hicks made the long drive west to fetch him, and by the time they arrived back in Seaford, the two were the best of friends. But with every other person he met, Nathan's behavior was exasperating. "Some poor woman came up on my porch to ask me where I got my porch swing, and all of the sudden, he was biting her," Hicks remembers.

Determined to show others what she saw in the dog, Hicks figured out that Nathan was food motivated, and an edible treat could dispel his hostility. When visitors arrived, Hicks would give them something tasty to feed him, and soon he was going for the treat rather than their ankles.

One evening after they had settled in together, Hicks got up from her desk to go to the kitchen, and when she returned, Nathan was standing up on his two back legs on her office chair, wiggling around as if he were dancing. Hicks grabbed her iPhone, filmed Nathan dancing, and sent the video to another volunteer, who suggested she add music. Soon, all Hicks had to do was to say "wiggle it," and Nathan would perform. Set to music like Macklemore and Ryan Lewis's "Thrift Shop" and Psy's "Gangnam Style," the videos went viral.

Six months into their foster relationship, Hicks thought Nathan was ready for adoption. She would mourn the loss of her dancing buddy, but she wasn't prepared to adopt a sixth pet for the long term. Hicks found what seemed like a perfect home for Nathan, with a groomer who was single and had another Chinese crested. But one week later, the groomer called Hicks and said she had changed her mind about having two dogs. She was giving Nathan up. She added that she thought he had already found the best home—with Hicks.

Refusing to put Nathan through yet another rehoming cycle, Hicks cut the dog a deal: "I will keep you," she remembers telling her spirited little friend. "But you have this talent, and you are going to use it to help other dogs get rescued." According to Hicks, Nathan has more than held up his end of the bargain.

Nathan—now known as Dancing Nathan—has spent years delighting fans with his antics, bringing attention to the breed and the rescue that finally found him a happy family life. "He's changing people's minds about the hairless breed," Hicks says. Contrary to some assumptions, he's not just an "ugly dog," she explains. "He's a cool dog that dances." The cool dog has also left behind his quarreling days—he's now far too busy boogying to bite. ◆

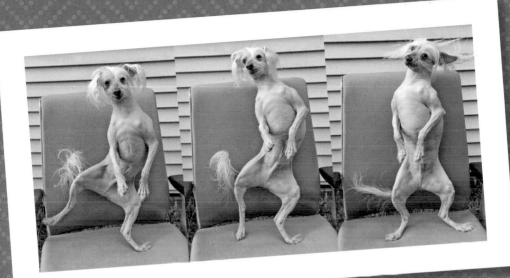

WHEN OWNER TINA HICKS (LEFT) DISCOVERED THAT HER JUMPING BEAN NATHAN WAS A DANCING SENSATION, SHE VOWED TO USE HIS INTERNET POPULARITY TO HELP OTHER RESCUE DOGS GET ADOPTED INTO LOVING FAMILIES.

FUR–EVER FAMILY: *Hamish was left all alone for extended periods of time before his new family found a spot for him in their heart and home—alongside their 28 other rescue animals.*

# HAMISH

## FINDING HIS PACK

### Shepherd mix ⬥ New York

Neil Abramson, an attorney who also does pro bono animal-welfare advocacy, considers himself the "no man." On the nine-acre property he shares with his family in upstate New York, he had capped their intake at 28 rescue animals, including five horses, a pig, a parrot, eight cats, four dogs, and what Abramson calls "the meanest rabbit alive."

But then he read about Hamish, a failed K9 left alone in his owners' empty second home; a volunteer walking him said the dog cried when she returned him to the uninhabited house. Days later, Hamish became the newest member of the Abramson family. Suffering from severe anxiety, Hamish wept when left alone. Abramson and his wife, veterinarian Amy Rodriguez, took turns sleeping beside him until he was finally able to sleep through the night.

Hamish is now a happy part of the accepting pack. The only holdout, according to Abramson, is the rabbit. As for his relationship with his savior: "He follows my wife everywhere, and he loves our kids. But he'll settle down with me if there's nobody else around." ◆

STORM SURVIVOR: *Rescued from abandonment after a hurricane, playful Charlotte was finally adopted and found a new family with the Animal Care and Control officers who rescued her.*

# CHARLOTTE

## ALONG FOR THE RIDE

### Mixed breed ⋈ North Carolina

Hurricane Matthew wreaked havoc throughout North Carolina, causing torrential rain and floods when it made landfall in October 2016. Charlotte-Mecklenburg Animal Care and Control (AC&C) officers dropped what they were doing and headed to hard-hit Edgecombe County. As they tended to dogs left behind in the chaos of the storm, one special canine started to become attached to them.

Under the usual protocol for storms, fieldwork officers would bring the dogs they found back to the Edgecombe shelter to be cared for until their owners might claim them. They would also perform care stops in which they would drop food and water to sustain the animals who were too afraid go with them.

In the harrowing aftermath of the storm, most of the local dogs were hesitant and withdrawn; but on one of their last days, Scott Kish, senior animal control enforcement officer, met a friendly little brown dog who was eager to play. When the team set out for the next care stop, the dog began to follow. The officers driving behind Kish began to film the dog as she trailed them for several blocks. The video shows her wagging her tail exuberantly and running to keep pace with the truck. Finally, Kish steps out and the dog jumps for joy.

Then, recalls Kish, she jumped into the passenger seat and snuggled up to his partner. "We knew we couldn't leave her there," he remembers.

Kish dropped the dog at the Edgecombe shelter, confident that her family would come to claim her. "She was so friendly that we knew that somebody owned her and had taken care of her," says Kish. The team uploaded their video to YouTube and it quickly spread across social media. Yet two months later, the AC&C said no one had claimed the dog, whom they'd named Charlotte after the city of her rescuers.

With a dog, cat, and an infant at home, Kish wasn't able to adopt Charlotte himself. But the department's spokesperson, Melissa Knicely, had an idea. The AC&C's eldest humane education canine was retiring, and from what she'd heard about Charlotte, she sounded like a stellar replacement. After consulting with the AC&C's humane education officer, Julia Conner, they decided that Charlotte not only had a new home but she also had a job.

## CHARLOTTE ALWAYS GREETS HIM WITH A WILDLY WAGGING TAIL AND KISSES—THANKS, PERHAPS, FOR THE RIDE OF HER LIFE.

Charlotte lives at Conner's with four other former shelter dogs whom she has trained; each dog belongs to the city and is assigned its own task of educating the public on proper animal care. The latest addition to the family adores her siblings: Rusty, a corgi–golden retriever mix, offers therapy at events and shelter tours; Wishbone, a Jack Russell terrier mix, participates in bite-prevention workshops with children; and Moya, a husky-Chihuahua–Staffordshire terrier mix does bite-prevention work with city employees, such as postal and gas workers, who often come into contact with unfamiliar dogs. Charlotte has stepped into the job from which a mixed breed named Ebony recently retired, working adoption and education events.

Conner's hardworking canines must have the endurance for an all-day event and the temperament to handle anything thrown at them. "Charlotte's a social butterfly," Conner describes. "She loves people, and she *loves* kids." Being the main attraction at an information booth is a natural fit for her.

Perhaps due to her experience during Hurricane Matthew, Charlotte still fears rain and storms, but she gets plenty of love to help her cope. On her way to or from an event, Charlotte often accompanies Conner to the shelter, where she has a chance to hang out with the man responsible for getting her the gig. "I'm not going to lie—it brought a tear to my eye that I couldn't take her," admits Kish. "But I know she is safe, and she is happy, and best of all, I can see her." Charlotte always greets him with a wildly wagging tail and kisses—thanks, perhaps, for the ride of her life. ◆

STROKE OF GENIUS: *Arbor is a quick learner—so quick, that her owner decided to train her to paint. Now, Arbor's art sells for more than $2,000 and raises funds and awareness for animal charities.*

# ARBOR

## TURNING RESCUE INTO
## AN ART FORM

### Mixed breed ⊶ Nevada

Even without words, Arbor is one of Las Vegas's strongest voices in animal-welfare activism. The striking mixed breed—part cattle dog, Australian border collie, Rottweiler, and German shepherd— raises awareness of dogs in need through her art and appearances at fund-raising events.

But it was Arbor's sweet nature and intelligence that first drew Bryce and Jennifer Henderson to her at the shelter—that, and the inky color of her coat, which the Hendersons knew put her at higher risk for euthanasia. As volunteers at local animal shelters, the couple had learned that black dogs are less likely to be adopted, a phenomenon known as black dog syndrome. So the Hendersons added Arbor to their family hoping to help change that trend, but they never expected that the dog would become a public sensation.

Arbor mastered basic obedience commands so quickly that after about six months, Jennifer decided to teach her a new skill: painting. Through positive reinforcement—one of Arbor's favorite rewards is a piece of broccoli offered every few brush strokes—Jennifer coached Arbor to hold a paintbrush in her mouth and apply paint to paper hung from an easel. One piece takes about half an hour to complete, and the results are bright and colorful abstract designs.

Soon, Arbor's work was selling for up to $2,100, with all proceeds going to animal charities. As the face of No Kill Las Vegas—a nonprofit watchdog organization that the Hendersons founded to monitor the practices of area shelters—Arbor uses her talents to advocate for canines in the system. The charming "Pawcasso" and spokes-dog has amassed a following of hundreds of thousands of fans on social media, and he turns out crowds by appearing at charity events. "We want to show that this is the kind of dog you can get at a shelter," Bryce says. "Your dog may not paint, but he or she will touch your life." ◆

ARBOR'S TALENTS HAVE HELPED RAISE AWARENESS OF SHELTER DOGS AND ABOUT THE SHELTER SYSTEM AT LARGE. SHE HAS LOTS OF FANS, WHO OFTEN SHOW UP IN CROWDS AT CHARITY EVENTS JUST TO SEE THE PAINTING PUP.

**CAPTAIN OF CONSERVATION:** *This pocket beagle, named Captain Ron, helps Disney scientists find at-risk sea turtle eggs buried on Florida's sandy beaches and teaches guests about conservation.*

# CAPTAIN RON

## A (CUTE) CASE
## FOR CONSERVATION

**Pocket beagle ⋈ Florida**

**M**arty MacPhee is familiar with every kind of cuteness out there, thanks in part to being a renowned expert on all things wild and curator of animal husbandry at Disney's Animal Kingdom theme park. So when it came time to put a face on Disney's conservation program, MacPhee knew they could do no better than a dog. "Dogs have a way of connecting people to issues on a completely different level than they might otherwise," says MacPhee.

The ideal dog would play two roles: wildlife detective and advocate for environmental protection issues. Disney scientists Anne Savage and Blair Witherington were hoping for a little help with their studies of sea turtles. They were spending long, hot days on a five-mile stretch of beach, searching for the eggs of leatherbacks, loggerheads, and green turtles, which might be buried beneath as much as two feet of sand. Once identified, the eggs were marked and protected from predators and human traffic, but it could take hours to find them—if they could be found at all. Says Savage, "We were wearing everybody out."

MacPhee called Pepe Peruyero, a dog trainer and former police officer who works with Disney. She explained that the dog in question would be asked to patrol the waterfront of Disney's Vero Beach Resort. The job requirements were all the more stringent given the employer—to match the carefully crafted fantasy of Disney World, the job demanded an even-tempered dog who could maintain composure while being grabbed at by children. Finally, she added the ultimatum: To represent Disney and charm the public, the dog had to be really, really, *really* cute.

Peruyero looked at the companion next to him and responded, "I've got the dog." Peruyero has spent nearly 20 years training detection dogs after he lost his beloved K9 partner, a German shepherd named Ross. When he decided he was ready to adopt again, he was drawn to the pocket beagle—so called because it is only about 13 inches long—for its diminutive size and vast intelligence. Captain Ron, named for the title character of the Kurt Russell comedy, had already proven to be an extraordinary pet. "He has the best qualities of all the dogs I've ever owned," says Peruyero. "He's loving and patient; he's fearless and protective and brilliant."

And Captain Ron was about to put those skills to the test as a working dog. Peruyero began training Captain Ron with specimens of mucus that the turtles secreted when they laid their eggs. "Normally it takes two to four weeks to get a dog imprinted on an odor," says the trainer. "It took Captain Ron 45 minutes."

Six weeks later, Peruyero and Captain Ron went to Vero Beach for a demonstration with Savage and Witherington. The night before the meeting, Peruyero took Captain Ron to the beach for the first time for a dress rehearsal. "He was totally freaked out by the waves, and I'm thinking, This is going to be a disaster," Peruyero remembers. But the next day, Captain Ron walked onto the beach,

AS SOON AS HANDLER PEPE PERUYERO (BELOW) BEGAN TO TRAIN CAPTAIN RON TO RECOGNIZE TURTLE EGGS BY SCENT, IT WAS CLEAR HE WAS A NATURAL (LEFT). NORMALLY DOGS TAKE TWO TO FOUR WEEKS TO IMPRINT ON A SCENT. IT TOOK CAPTAIN RON 45 MINUTES.

greeted everyone, and began alerting. It normally takes a person 25 minutes to find the turtle eggs; Captain Ron was finding them in 30 seconds.

Savage and Witherington led Captain Ron to known nest sites as well as "false crawls"—spots where turtles have begun digging but ultimately did not lay eggs. The shrewd detection dog performed with a 100 percent accuracy rate, alerting to eggs in the real nests and showing no interest in the false ones. "What was really fun was pitting Blair, who has 30 years of experience, against the dog," Savage says. "Captain Ron did better—I'm just saying."

**IT NORMALLY TAKES A PERSON 25 MINUTES TO FIND THE TURTLE EGGS; CAPTAIN RON WAS FINDING THEM IN 30 SECONDS.**

Working three months of the year, Captain Ron's accuracy has remained perfect, despite what MacPhee says is a slightly less-than-perfect work ethic. "Captain Ron isn't like, 'I wanna I wanna I wanna' like some working dogs," she says with a laugh. "He's more like, "Pepe, let's go spend some time on the beach!" The playful pet has been known to run down the beach chasing a cute female dog or two; but of the mischief-making, MacPhee adds: "I dare anyone to have a bad day if Ron is anywhere nearby."

That uplifting spirit has translated into Captain Ron's job as a conservation ambassador. As part of the park's outreach programs, the charismatic beagle performs meet and greets and stars in in-room videos and public talks. He reminds guests to turn the lights off when they leave a room, hang up their towels so they can be reused, and recycle plastic bottles—conservation acts that he demonstrates himself. When Captain Ron is on stage accompanying a talk on the importance of recycling, people are more likely to remember the message, says Peruyero, thanks to the dog's unique and memorable performance. The charming pup is embracing life as a Disney diplomat as much as the community has embraced him—a setup that delights the conservation team.

Thanks to Captain Ron's success in detection, Peruyero received the green light to train Dory, a second Disney rescue dog, who searches for gopher tortoises as well as sea turtle eggs. "On many beaches, if the eggs aren't found and protected, they are destroyed," says Witherington. "It's nice to think about this 'technology' we developed being used to help conservation in those places." Captain Ron has saved thousands of sea turtle eggs so far. It's an impressive tally that makes him an expert conservationist—and certainly one of the cutest. ◆

# RESOURCES

### Alliance of Therapy Dogs
Cheyenne, WY
therapydogs.com
307-432-0272
office@therapydogs.com

### Animal Medical Clinic of Goose Creek
Goose Creek, SC
amcgoose.com
843-569-3647
info@amcgoose.com

### Animal Wellness Clinic
Michigan City, IN
animalwellnessclinic.com
219-872-0661

### Arizona Animal Welfare League & SPCA
Phoenix, AZ
aawl.org
602-273-6852

### Bald Is Beautiful
Greenville, SC
baldisbeautifuldogrescue.org
baldisbeautifuldogrescue@gmail.com

### Companions for Courage
Clermont, FL
companionsforcourage.org
352-602-3428
info@companionsforcourage.org

### Cuyahoga County Animal Shelter
Valley View, OH
cuyahogadogs.com
216-525-7877

### Domesti-PUPS
Lincoln, NE
domesti-pups.org
402-465-4201
info@domesti-pups.org

**Fred Says**
Chicago, IL
fredsays.org
773-303-6058

**Freshfields Animal Rescue**
Liverpool, UK
freshfields.org.uk
+44 151-931-1604
admin@freshfields.org.uk

**Funds for Furry Friends**
Brandon, MB, Canada
fundsfurfriends.com
204-573-8333
adoptions@fundsfurfriends.com

**Italian Greyhound Rescue of the Gulf Coast**
igrescuegulfcoast.org
662-883-0845
igrescuegulfcoast@gmail.com

**K9s For Warriors**
Ponte Vedra Beach, FL
K9sforwarriors.org
904-686-1956
info@k9sforwarriors.org

**Leashes of Valor**
Sparta, VA
leashesofvalor.org
904-502-4025
info@leashesofvalor.org

**No Kill Las Vegas**
Las Vegas, NV
nklv.org

**Operation Pets Alive!**
The Woodlands, TX
operationpetsalive.org
info@operationpetsalive.org

**Plenty of Pit Bulls**
Gainesville, FL
popb.org
352-405-1696
gainesvillepitbulls@gmail.com

**Universal K9**
San Antonio, TX
universalk9inc.com
210-858-6830
info@universalk9inc.com

# ILLUSTRATIONS CREDITS

Cover, Kaylee Greer/Dog Breath Photography; 1, Mike Mezeul II; 2–3, Michelangelo Oprandi/Dreamstime; 4, Elizabeth Spence—@wellettas on Instagram; 7, Michele Romero; 8, Courtesy of the Cincinnati Zoo; 11 (UP), AP Photo/John Minchillo; 11 (LO), Courtesy of the Cincinnati Zoo; 12, Jimena Suárez; 15 (UP), Ira Block; 15 (LO), Jordi Serqueda—@serqueda on Instagram; 16, Debra Guajardo; 19 (UP), Jesse Bullinger; 19 (LO), Brad Croft; 22, Miki Hirabayashi; 25 (UP), Miki Hirabayashi; 25 (LO), Courtesy of Makoto Kumagai; 26, Brianna Paciorka/Knoxville News-Sentinel; 28–31, Courtesy of Marley's Mutts Dog Rescue; 32–5, Debra Garrett; 36, Francis Gardler/Lincoln Journal Star; 39 (UP), Francis Gardler/Lincoln Journal Star; 39 (LO), Jenny Inness; 42, Terri Spaeth-Merrick; 45 (UP), Invictus Detection Dogs; 45 (LO), The Canadian Press/Darryl Dyck; 46, Freshfields Animal Rescue, www.freshfields.org.uk; 51 (UP), Freshfields Animal Rescue, www.freshfields.org.uk; 51 (LO), MEN Media; 52, Nicole Valint; 56, Christy Borgstedte @ CLB Photography, staging courtesy Ninth Circuit Court of Florida; 60, Chris LaChall/Courier-Post; 62–5, Mike Mezeul II; 66, Karen Presecan Photography, courtesy of Jason Haag; 69 (LE), Araya Diaz/Getty Images for American Humane Association; 69 (RT), K9s For Warriors, courtesy of Jason Haag; 70 (UP), Karen Presecan Photography, courtesy of Jason Haag; 70 (LO), Leigh Vogel/Getty Images for A+E; 72, Keith Barraclough Photography, courtesy of TurfMutt; 75 (BOTH), Jeff Mauritzen, courtesy of TurfMutt; 76, Courtesy of Cuyahoga County Animal Shelter; 80, Holly Sanger; 82, Linda Orlowski-Smith; 85 (UP), Courtesy of Linda Orlowski-Smith; 85 (LO), Linda Orlowski-Smith; 86, Stacey Morrison/Happy Tails Pet Photography; 89 (UP), Tara Walton/Toronto Star via Getty Images; 89 (LO), Stacey Morrison/Happy Tails Pet Photography; 92–5, Elizabeth Spence—@wellettas on Instagram; 96, Christopher Shane; 99 (LE), Christopher Shane; 99 (RT), William Lindler; 100, Chris Bauer; 103 (UP), Chris Bauer; 103 (LO), Timmy Samuel/Starbelly Studios; 106, © 2017 Pawsitively Priceless Pet Photography; 109 (UP), Courtesy of Courtney Ivan/Elite EMS; 109 (LO), © 2017 Pawsitively Priceless Pet Photography; 110, JoAnna Platzer; 112, Mike Walzak; 116–19, Courtney Dasher—@tunameltsmyheart on Instagram; 120–25, Courtesy of Gibran Andrawos; 126, Connie Summers Photography; 129 (UP), Suncoast Pet Magazine; 129 (LO), Connie Summers Photography; 130, Courtesy of Meridith and Jack Doucette; 133 (UP), Courtesy of Meridith and Jack Doucette; 133 (LO), Courtesy of Arizona Animal Welfare League; 136–9 (UP), 39design; 139 (LO), Carmen Doherty Photography; 140, Dr. Amy Rodriguez; 142, Charlotte-Mecklenburg Police Department Animal Care & Control; 146–9, Bryce and Jen Henderson; 150–53, John Fulton; back cover, John Fulton.

Illustrations by Katie Olsen, NG Staff

Since 1888, the National Geographic Society has funded more than 12,000 research, exploration, and preservation projects around the world. National Geographic Partners distributes a portion of the funds it receives from your purchase to National Geographic Society to support programs including the conservation of animals and their habitats.

National Geographic Partners
1145 17th Street NW
Washington, DC 20036-4688 USA

Become a member of National Geographic and activate your benefits today at natgeo.com/jointoday.

For information about special discounts for bulk purchases, please contact National Geographic Books Special Sales: specialsales@natgeo.com

For rights or permissions inquiries, please contact National Geographic Books Subsidiary Rights: bookrights@natgeo.com

ISBN: 978-1-4262-1906-1

Printed in China
17/RRDS/1

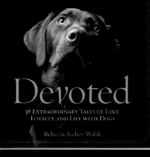